HAWAII GOES TO WAR

HAWAII GOES TO WAR

LIFE IN HAWAII FROM PEARL HARBOR TO PEACE

by
DeSoto Brown

DESIGN
by
Anne Ellett

Editions Limited

Copyright© DeSoto Brown, 1989

Published by:
Editions Limited
111 Royal Circle
Honolulu, Hawaii 96816
Gaylord H. Wilcox and David A. Rick

All page layouts and typesetting
produced on computer by:
Wishing Printing
1F Wah Ha Factory Building
8 Shipyard Lane
Quarry Bay, Hong Kong
Fax: 5658351

First Edition, October 1989

ISBN 0-915013-11-8 Hardcover
      0-915013-12-6 Softcover

Printed in Hong Kong

TABLE OF CONTENTS

H - 283 Yachts, Pearl Harbor

Pearl Harbor presents a serene
picture in this postcard from the
late 1930s.

"...Hawaii is a big consideration in contemplation of any Pacific war possibilities...

Says one 'school of guessing': The Japanese might get a number of aircraft carriers within a few hundred miles of Honolulu, then swoop over the city...and drop bombs on forts, barracks, government buildings... Possibly!...Not too probable!

In the first place: The Island of Oahu...is rather well equipped defensively as to enemy air reception...and ever is alert and watchful (as a matter of military routine, not that anything of the sort is expected or should be expected...) In the second place...what would it profit Japan?...

Time...would prove a Honolulu attack vain and wasteful of effort, and inviting reactions tremendous."

Paradise of the Pacific magazine, January 1936

PRELUDE

The Fleet's In

During the 1920s and '30s, the United States fleet was still based on the West Coast, and when it came to Hawaii on manuevers there was cause for celebration. The average citizen got a chance to view an exciting show as the great ships anchored offshore, and the merchants of Honolulu and Lahaina enjoyed increased sales of everything from liquor to souvenirs as sailors swarmed into town on leave.

But behind the fun and frolics of shore leave was the real reason for the Navy being here: to test and demonstrate new techniques of offensive and defensive warfare. Not so incidentally, this served also to show other nations the strength and abilities of the United States military.

Facing page, far right: Visiting sailors could buy cheesy postcards like these to commemorate their time in the islands. *Near right:* One of the delights of shore leave: an ukulele lesson given by Phyllis Maple on the sands of Waikiki; May 13, 1935. A somber note to this carefree scene - the sailor at far left is a crew member of the USS Arizona, at this point six years away from its tragic destiny as the eventual symbol of the Pearl Harbor attack.

Previous pages: Army searchlights at Fort DeRussy silhouette thc Royal Hawaiian and Moana Hotels at Waikiki in the 1930s.

"ALOHA HAWAII"

"I'll go but I'm not buying anything."

"HAWAIIAN MANEUVERS"

Our Nation's Military Might

As the 1930s progressed, an increasingly tense international situation created an obvious, growing military presence in Hawaii. For example, those who might doubt the resources of the USA could be reassured by one of the showy reviews regularly put on for the public at Schofield Barracks. These were vast and inspiring things, befitting what was the nation's largest military base. One such presentation in 1939 showed off trucks, tanks, machine guns, field artillery, ten thousand marching troops, and even carrier pigeons - and it all took more than an hour to pass in front of the 7,000 spectators in the stands. Another popular and highly visible display of strength in the 1930s from both the Army and Navy: searchlight shows over Pearl Harbor and other locations.

In spite of all this, most mainlanders remained unaware of Hawaii's crucial military role; many probably didn't even know Hawaii was a part of the United States at all. A poll taken by *Fortune* magazine in 1939 disclosed that less than 73% of those questioned would want to go to war if a foreign country attacked Hawaii; this was fewer than the amount who would defend Canada.

Above: Part of the impressive arsenal at Schofield Barracks - the 13th Field Artillery in 1938. ***Upper right:*** Searchlights sweep the sky over Pearl Harbor in the mid 1930s.

The Japanese Question

術合居部道劍

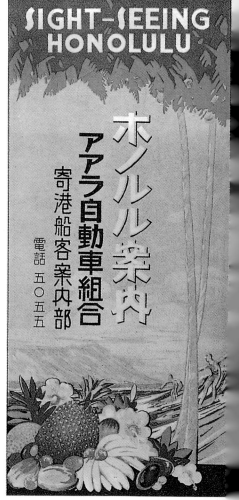

SIGHT-SEEING HONOLULU

ホノルル案内
アアラ自動車組合
寄港船客案内部
電話 五〇五五

The Japanese were by far the most numerous element in prewar Hawaii's multi-racial population, and an abundance of Japanese schools, clubs, movie theaters, and religious institutions made this fact obvious. Even though a good percentage of these people were American citizens, their presence in the islands was, to many people - especially visiting journalists - cause for alarm.

Starting in 1931, Japan had become increasingly aggressive throughout Asia, and had charged into an outright and particularly brutal war against China in 1937. The United States condemned this war, but some local Japanese residents were known to support it. Where did such people's sympathies ultimately lie?

The Japanese, to a number of onlookers, seemed mysteriously clannish and prone to stick to their own kind, and their ties to the homeland seemed especially strong. Many still spoke Japanese, a language few others knew, and over 40,000 of their children attended hundreds of special schools throughout the islands to continue to study it. But what else was this younger generation learning? Were they also being indoctrinated with loyalty to the Emperor of Japan?

If so, and if Japan's militaristic expansion were to reach Hawaii...could the local Japanese be trusted?

Above left: Three teachers in martial arts garb pictured in the 1940 yearbook of the Moiliili Japanese School. *Above* and *facing page:* Signs of Japanese influence in Hawaii in the 1930s: a promotional guidebook and a downtown Honolulu movie theater.

Fort Street – Honolulu, Hawaii

"War may be near in the Pacific, but worry about it - until it comes - will simply have to wait until Mr. and Mrs. Hawaii get through with...celebrating the greatest festive season of the year."

Honolulu, T. H., 1941

World War II did not begin in December 1941 in Hawaii. It had actually been going on for years by then, in Europe and Asia, and in the islands the tension of war's possible arrival had risen and fallen repeatedly.

Throughout Hawaii's last year of peace, residents were told of measures being taken to protect them should war strike. Medical supplies were laid in, blood plasma was banked, and stocks of food were gathered with housewives being specifically ordered to buy up a supply for their own homes. Meanwhile, committees representing business, government, and the military all met, planned, and took first aid lessons. This was all extensively publicized, but even so, people were still not completely convinced that the war could touch them. There were wildly opposing views on the subject, as these two quotes from *Hawaii* magazine illustrate. One writer thought *"...the world situation has grown on us gradually until actual entry into active combat will not come as very much of a shock. This much we may as well resign ourselves to: We are going to take an active, fighting part in this war; soon!"* Another wrote a few months later: *"Threats of 'drastic action' if the democracies persisted in their 'encircling of Japan' have proven pure bluff...Japan is no longer a menace to*

the United States...[its] sun is heading into almost total eclipse." Who were you to believe?

Confronted with such contradictions, Honolulu residents usually ended up thinking about the more immediate problems they faced, like the influx of mainland defense workers which was pushing rents and traffic accidents up, and (more mundanely) a controversial plan for one-way streets downtown. The good news was that the economy was doing well, with a healthy picture for Hawaii's agricultural mainstays, sugar and pineapple. Tourism boomed; most other places were too tense - or impossible - to visit, and Hawaii seemed out of harm's way. *"You will be able to realize the real pleasures of a crossing on world-famous ships, Hawaii bound, **over peaceful seas**,"* emphasized an ad in *Paradise of the Pacific* magazine's December 1941 issue. As a year of conflicting good and bad news neared its close, islanders wondered what might come next - but hoped for the best.

Above: Honolulu goes about its daily business - looking down Fort Street on a busy afternoon in 1941. *Left:* [On November 29] *"Fort Street was set ablaze with Christmas lights, inaugurating what will no doubt be Honolulu's...merriest Christmas on record." Right:* Unknowingly prophetic - but exactly one week too soon - is the top headline of the Nov. 30, 1941 *Honolulu Advertiser.* But the "strike" mentioned in the headline was expected to be elsewhere in the Pacific - and besides, there had been scare headlines like this all year...

ATTACK!

ATTACK!
December 7th, 1941

"At the outset, we, and probably a great many other people, thought the military were carrying on a maneuver. Many people gathered out in the streets and craned their necks to watch the 'show.'"

It might seem dramatically wrong to refer to the morning of December 7th, 1941 as "peaceful." Yet, until a few minutes before 8:00 a.m., that is exactly what it was. When explosions rattled windows and smoke billowed in the distance, most of those who could see what was going on just did not accept the possibility that they were watching an earthshaking historical event.

"'Smoke bombs!'...my friend said disgustedly. 'Maneuvers were supposed to have ended Friday...!'"

"...I believed...[this] was nothing to become alarmed over, though I had to admit it was very realistic."

"'There is only one thing wrong with this. If the real thing should ever happen people might think they were crying "wolf" and not respond.'"

"This looked real yet we still couldn't believe it."

Above: A Japanese "Val" over Pearl Harbor. *Below:* The view from Aiea of the destruction. *Right:* Honolulu civilians gaze at what they think is a make-believe air battle.

Previous pages: A scene in the sky over Pearl Harbor.

"As soon as we would get one house empty, the roof would be in flames...at least two-thirds of the block burned to the ground..."

ATTACK!

December 7th, 1941

Those who were not able to really believe that a war was beginning were convinced if they were near the intersection of King and McCully Streets, for this was the site of Honolulu's biggest civilian fire on the morning of the attack. Firefighters were mostly tied up assisting with the tremendous blazes at the military bases and could not respond quickly enough, or in large enough numbers, to save 13 buildings here from destruction.

"There was no fire apparatus in sight. A high wind carried the flames to the rear and ewa side of the stores. There was little we could do...After twenty minutes of this, one piece of fire apparatus came screaming down King Street..."

For 31 families this meant the loss of their homes, but a few managed to save something.

"About 11:30 a.m as I went to the store next door to shop, [an anti-aircraft shell] fell...Soon after a fire was raging and I helped move our things as well as our neighbor's across the street to safety...the whole block including my house was burned down...I was very much in [grief.]"

Most tragic of all - death. The fate of Mrs. Kisa Hatate of 944 McCully St. (one of 4 who perished in the area) was described by her brother: *"...a shell...pierced the side wall of the basement...the exploding fragments flew up and hit my sister on the leg...[another brother] rushed her to the hospital, but she probably died on the way...from loss of blood. By the time [he] returned...the house was completely destroyed by fire. Not a single thing was saved as the fire spread too rapidly."*

These sad, charred remains were not removed until October 1942, and wartime shortages of building materials meant life could not really return until April 1944, when the first new home appeared.

Facing page: Reminders of damaged lives: scorched barber chairs and a bedspring from a second floor apartment, among sheets of corrugated metal roofing. *Below:* On McCully Street, residents gather belongings hastily pulled from the burned out area and prepare to find shelter somewhere else.

ATTACK!
December 7th, 1941

Burning debris blown by the tradewinds from the fire at King and McCully Streets (pp. 22-23) spread flames to the Lunalilo School, a few blocks away on Pumehana Street. No one was in school that day, of course, but a Red Cross aid station had already been set up in the building to attend to early attack casualties. Out they all went, to be cared for on benches on the school grounds, while boys and men grabbed what they could from inside.

Assisting in this effort, as well as the larger fire at King and McCully, were members of the American Legion. Called by radio announcements to their clubhouse (at McCully and Kapiolani Boulevard, just blocks from the fires) 75 to 100 men reported: *"...a few [men] were endeavoring to organize a controlling body out of an apparent unorganized milling crowd within the building... [finally] some semblance of order follow[ed]. Phone calls came in for details for guarding the wharfs etc....night guards were furnished for the City reservoirs and wharves."*

Not only the American Legion volunteered to do whatever was necessary; people all over the island rushed to help drive makeshift ambulances, nurse the wounded, and guard important facilities of all kinds. In the first hectic days some found themselves working for tremendous stretches without sleep or food, and sometimes men keeping watch in lonely locations were unintentionally abandoned when no one showed up to relieve them. But such mistakes would become fewer as things got better organized.

Above: Nurses on the march next to Lunalilo School; fire has driven them outdoors. *Facing page:* Desks, shelves, bulletin boards, a litter of papers - and an American flag - are all piled on the lawn of the burning Lunalilo School.

ATTACK!
December 7th, 1941

War? No, it couldn't be! [That] was something that happened in far off places." Even with the obvious going on all around, there was still strong disbelief on many people's part. For one thing, military manuevers had been going on for more than the past year, often not too dissimilar to what they were seeing this morning.

"It must be a practice alert and to make it more real our boys have painted the Rising Sun insignia on their planes."

"I ran over to Central Union Church...[and] told one old gentleman what I had heard over the radio and saw over Pearl Harbor. His reply was this: 'It is only the Navy giving us a scare, but I think they are carrying it too far.'"

"If those are only manuevers, they're playing awfully rough this morning."

But such attitudes were rudely changed by reality. Continuing destruction could not be ignored.

"It was hard to watch helplessly and see the destruction being done. It was hard to realize Hawaii was at war. It was a nightmare!"

The truth of the situation, awful as it was, did not affect all observers equally. One Boy Scout's memory of the day was that *"We* were going to have a ball game in the morning but due to the Japanese raid we had to call it off."

Dramatic proof that this was not "manuevers."
Facing page: An errant American anti-aircraft shell
landed directly on this parked automobile on
Channel Street near Honolulu Harbor. (In the
backround is the Honolulu Iron Works on South
Street.) *Above:* More damage: the Paul Goo home on
Liliha Street near Kuakini.

**"Dressed for Sunday School, my sister and I
were on our way when suddenly a missile
hurtled past above us...and imbedded itself in
the side of a house. Too stunned to move, I saw
people rushing out of their houses to view the
shattered structure, while the owner of the
house ...gestured wildly to the sky..."**

ATTACK!
December 7th, 1941

Anti-aircraft shells fired by Americans at Pearl Harbor and other military posts were, of course, supposed to explode high in the air to destroy Japanese planes. Normally this would be accomplished by setting a fuse to time the projectile's detonation. But in the disorganization of the sudden attack, fuses were being set incorrectly or not at all, and some shells were defective as well. Those same shells eventually came back to earth intact - but they didn't remain in that state when they hit. Some did little damage, like the ones that struck Diamond Head or fell into the sea. But at least 40 landed in scattered sites all over Honolulu, where the explosions were assumed to be Japanese bombs. In reality, the enemy's ammunition was meant for military targets almost exclusively, far from Honolulu. Any civilian destruction that day was secondary to Japan's purpose.

Above: A group of civilian men - and one National Guardsman - examine a crater in the lawn of Washington Place, the Governor's mansion near downtown Honolulu. *Facing page:* Yet more damage, this time in the heart of Waikiki, in the middle of Lewers Road just mauka of Kuhio Avenue.

"...toward Waikiki Beach I saw a bomb strike what appeared to be a new apartment house...No fire started but there was a huge cloud of dust or smoke...It developed later that the bomb struck in the street just outside [the] apartment, shattering all windows..."

ATTACK!
December 7th, 1941

"I saw the car that had been [hit]. It was a horrible sight...worst of all was the interior...Blood was spattered all over the seats. Just looking at it made me feel sick and angry."

More than 300 Oahu civilian residents were hurt that day and of those, at least 57 died (an exact count is not known.) Many ended up at Queen's Hospital, Honolulu's largest medical facility. Among the injured, nurses there recalled a Japanese family of three who were all hurt at the same time and whose brother was killed, an old lady strafed while she was walking to church, a little oriental girl *"who had her arm hanging in shreds,"* three different women who each had an arm amputated, and a man who died after *"his whole back had been shot away."*

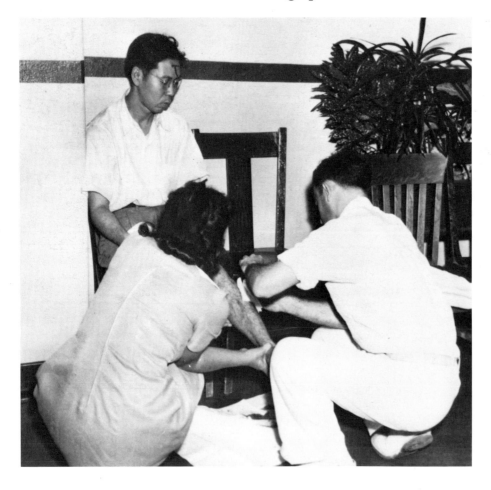

Left: An injured civilian's leg is bandaged at Queen's Hospital. (The letter T on his forehead means he's received a tetanus shot.) To add to the confusion at Queen's, the elevators lost power and some patients had to be hoisted up to the higher floors by a pulley on the outside of the building.

Above: John Adams slumps lifeless at the wheel of his 1937 Packard. Also dead in the car are his father Joseph and another passenger, Joseph McCabe. All three Kaneohe residents were on the way to their jobs at Pearl Harbor when they were killed by a projectile opposite 802 Judd Street in the Liliha district.

ATTACK!
December 7th, 1941

"Thank God for the radio!"

Broadcasting proved its worth that day. People turned to their radios for information - and support, in a time of fear.

At first, things continued as usual on Honolulu's two stations, with only a few short announcements for military personnel to report for duty. These noncommittal statements said nothing of an attack. But people could see what was going on and wanted to know what it meant. One woman was frightened:

*"'My God!' I thought. 'It's war!' and swiftly turned on the radio. The tubes hummed. It seemed a terribly long time to me...and then a church service came over the air [**First Baptist Church of Waikiki** on KGMB]. I tried our other local station and got a Japanese program [**Plantation Airs** on KGU]...I was reassured, yet still with some misgivings."*

The first real verification of the attack didn't come until 8:40 (more that forty minutes after the war had started) when KGMB interrupted a transcribed show of the Salt Lake Tabernacle Choir, then in the midst of a hymn whose chorus ironically repeated, "All is well, all is well." Announcer Webley Edwards made sure there was no doubt in listeners' minds by forcefully stating that what was going on

was not a practice but "the real McCoy!" - a phrase destined for immediate fame.

"When I heard the KGU announcer say, 'We are under attack - do not use the phone...keep calm - the situation is under control,'...[my husband] said 'Manuevers.' I tuned to KGMB and heard the announcer say the same thing, so I said...in a very grave tone 'This is the real thing. This is war.'"

Regular programming stopped. *Friendly Gospel Hour* and *Army Navy Sports Review* were among the scheduled shows that would never be heard; instead, emergency announcements took their place, interspersed with music ranging from "Three Little Fishies" to "The Star-Spangled Banner."

"The announcer...kept telling us to be calm but he didn't sound any too calm himself."

"The radio station seemed to be in a state of confusion, for we could hear disturbing noises from the movement of furniture and people as music was being played..."

"The Governor came on the air and the poor fellow was so nervous he could scarcely speak..."

Just as Governor Poindexter was finishing his declaration of a state of emergency at 11:41, all local stations were ordered to stop broadcasting for fear that more Japanese

attackers might use them to be guided to the islands. Then there was only the police radio to listen to (most home sets could receive such broadcasts then) as it sent out orders to officers:

"Investigate Japanese at 781 Sunset Avenue...proceed to St. Louis Heights; parachutists supposed to have landed...arrest that man - bring him down here - he is an imposter..." One young man thought that *"These [police] reports certainly didn't help any, for they only added more to the perplexity that already existed."*

The commercial stations were forced to stay off the air for the whole following week *"except for occasional messages & instructions. We were to leave the radio on...all day in case an important message came over - wonder we didn't burn out all our tubes ---"*

Unfortunately, this silence came just when people were hungriest for news. The only reports - or entertainment, which everyone needed too - that anyone could get were short wave mainland broadcasts that *"usually die out just when you most want to hear them."*

Still, it was better than nothing.

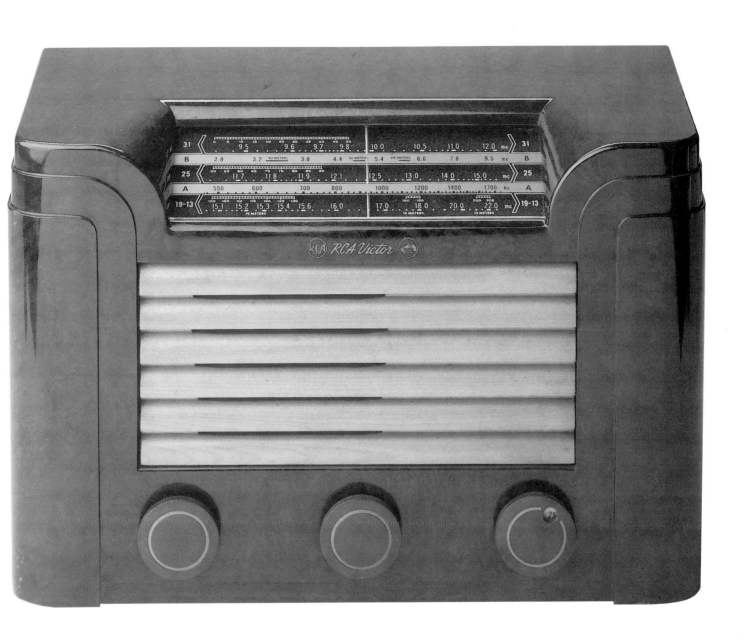

Above: The complicated dial of this 1941 RCA Victor table model radio shows how island residents could tune in local police calls and even mainland broadcasts, both crucial on Dec. 7th and just after.

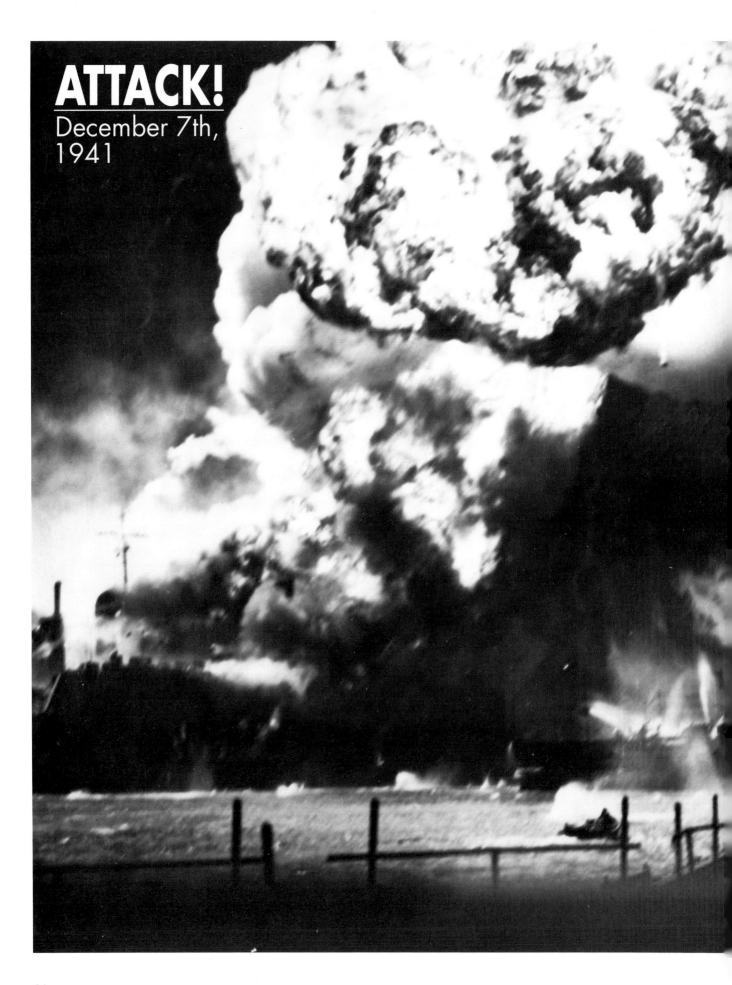

ATTACK!
December 7th,
1941

Watching the attack from far away, civilians were fearful but most didn't feel directly threatened. Not so for those who lived "next door" to military bases - or were actually there. Residents close to the action quickly understood what was happening, and many fled. One young girl, crammed into a car with evacuating relatives, realized to her shock that she was now an actual war refugee - just like the ones she'd seen in photographs from other parts of the world.

Wives and children of service personnel who lived on base at Pearl Harbor suddenly found themselves in real danger. A woman remembered the near-panic in one housing area:

"...most of the women were...upset and nervous, in fact almost hysterical...various runners kept moving from house to house, giving contradicting orders. One Marine gave orders for all women to stay in their houses, promptly followed by another who went through and called to people to come out in the streets and lie flat."

The men who were actually in the midst of the bombs and bullets at Pearl Harbor had no advice on what to do. They were trying to just stay alive in the face of the chaotic terror of torpedoes, burning fuel, and deadly shrapnel.

Left: The explosion of the USS Shaw was one of the largest of the tremendous blows at Pearl Harbor on December 7th and occurred near the end of the attack. *"Then...was the spectacle that was the crowning achievement of this sneak attack. The USS SHAW was bombed and burning up. [Blown] up by her own magazines. All hell had broken loose that day. More hell than can be imagined..."*
Below: Smoke boils up from beyond the officers' quarters at Pearl Harbor.

ATTACK!
December 7th, 1941

"It was too late to find shelter, bombs were falling all over. Every building was a potential target. Best that I stay in the open offering only a small target to the enemy."

Above: A bomb blasted this crater in a street at Hickam Field, still shrouded with smoke at 4:40 in the afternoon of December 7th. *Facing page:* Men load a wounded sailor into a pick-up truck serving as an emergency ambulance, probably at Kaneohe Naval Air Station.

Even such "small targets" were hit, though - about 3,500 of them. Wounded men were dispatched to military hospitals in whatever vehicles could be found, including delivery trucks from Honolulu businesses that answered calls broadcast on the radio.

"...an ambulance had just come in. Men were carrying stretchers back and forth...I was so frightened...One injured man's face was all charred...another man was screaming and others were just moaning."

Some of the wounded were unexpectedly stoical. One lieutenant at Tripler Hospital calmly remarked to a nurse, *"I sure would hate to lose that leg."* Another man, hearing the screams of a nearby patient being operated on without anesthetic, said *"I don't mind all these things but that gets me"* - even though the speaker was more severely hurt.

ATTACK!
December 7th, 1941

"...we began noticing cars tearing past us...as we got to the Kailua Junction we saw clouds of black smoke billowing up from Mokapu."

The disaster on December 7th was immediately referred to as simply "Pearl Harbor," a sort of verbal shorthand to cover the events of the entire day. Certainly the harbor itself bore the brunt of the tragedy, but four other Oahu military bases (and nearby civilian areas) were attacked as well, and all suffered destruction and death.

Hickam Field (next to Pearl Harbor), Kaneohe Naval Air Station on the Mokapu Peninsula on the windward side, Wheeler Field at Schofield Barracks in central Oahu, and Bellows Field at Waimanalo painfully felt war's arrival. In Waipahu, Ewa, and Wahiawa, the Japanese took some time from their main objectives to strafe whatever else lay in range; in these towns and sugar plantations, civilians were injured and killed.

About 360 Japanese planes were in the air over Oahu that morning. Arriving by complete surprise gave them an almost unbeatable advantage; only 29 were shot down by frustrated Americans.

"The marines were firing...with rifles, machine guns and some with pistols at...planes diving down on Hickam Field."

The low-level maneuvering of the marauding aircraft left a strong impression:

"A single Jap plane flew...a few feet above the trees and I not only saw the plane...but the pilot and his goggles."

Many people reported clearly viewing the enemy pilots through the clear canopies of their aircraft in the same way - and never forgot it.

The attack was over with, for the most part, by about 9:45 am. Almost all of the enemy planes were gone. Amazingly, this catastrophe had occurred in only about two hours...but these were hours that literally changed the world.

Ahead was the United States' full-on plunge into World War II.

Right: A 1941 Dodge sedan bearing military personnel races towards flaming ruins at Kaneohe Naval Air Station, where 27 planes and 2 hangars were destroyed.

ATTACK!
Aftermath

Seen in the entire tragic sweep of World War II, the 2,335 fatalities of December 7th are a comparatively small number, even for a single battle; but for Hawaii they represented a disaster on a scale never seen before. For the United States, and indeed the rest of the world, the numbers alone cannot fully signify the meaning of the attack and its effect on history.

President Roosevelt declared January 1, 1942 to be a national day of prayer. On that day, thousands of Honolulu residents *"from all walks of life...came, with their floral tributes"* to a memorial service at Oahu Cemetery for 328 Navy men (and 13 of the Japanese attackers) buried there. (In later years, all of these remains would be moved to other locations - and the Japanese would return home.)

"...the USS ARIZONA. Sunk to the bottom. Blasted by enemy torpedoes and bombs...coffin for hundreds of brothers, husbands and sweethearts..."

Below: Seen from Ford Island, the USS Arizona, its superstructure still above water, continues to burn on December 8th. Over 1,000 men remained on board - nearly half of all those killed in the attack. *Right:* At Oahu Cemetery, a singing troupe from the Daughters of Hawaii bids goodbye to the dead of December 7th with *Aloha Oe*.

Previous pages: The tragedy of the attack: a Navy man lies dead in now-quiet waters at the Kaneohe Naval Air Station.

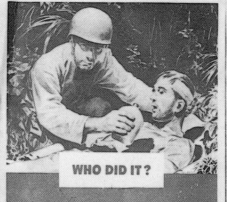

HOMEFRONT HAWAII

The Shock of War

Yesterday seems centuries away." In the space of just one day, life had been turned upside down. December 8th brought new problems and fears.

"Most stores are closed...People knocked off work early. Everyone still amazed...Can't begin to describe Honolulu... Somber, still stunned, hollow. Only a sprinkling of people on the streets. Windows boarded up or taped...precaution against shattering glass."

There were hints of panic. Most people's first thought was to procure things they needed. They knew that shipping from the mainland was likely to be disrupted, if not cut off completely.

"There was a great demand for medical supplies...paper tape, gasoline, groceries, etc. Many of these items were unobtainable..."

The main goal was to lay in a stock of food.

"Lines had formed at all grocery stores and there was a mad rush as...people tried to buy everything on the shelves...that day the jitters were fast catching up with me..."

"I went down to May's [Market]...only a few were allowed to go in at a time..."

"The queues were long everywhere. I waited one hour at Piggly Wiggly."

For some, there was a sense of helplessness. The future was impossible to guess - except that it looked bad. "...our world was crumbling all around us. Would it ever be like the old happy carefree days...!"

Those who knew what the attack had done to the military had cause for fear. They knew that if the Japanese were to return soon, not much could be done in defense.

"'It's unbelievable...From what I hear...they've wiped us out. They've knocked us flat. We've nothing left to fight with.'"

Facing page: Shoppers wait to be admitted to the Kaimuki Super Market to purchase only a "normal" amount of food (meaning no hoarding.) *"...the food stores can only sell to their regular customers and then in limited quantities."*

Previous pages: Two Island women look over a wallful of typical World War II posters, most of them issued locally.

Top: "Andrade's on Fort Street has already blossomed out with a huge red and blue 'V.'" *Above:* "...windows... have been taped...Some patterns are artistic; others are designed for more practical purposes." In spite of the seriousness of the situation, these downtown workers smile for the camera.

"The first week after the [attack] was quite dismal. People were stunned and bewildered..."

The Debris of War

The debris of war littered Oahu. Live ammunition would continue to be discovered for many years, and some of it would take lives when handled carelessly; two Ewa Plantation workers were killed by a shell one found in a field in March 1942. But most of these objects could no longer cause harm, like the remains of some of the 29 Japanese planes that were shot down, and the chunks of shrapnel many gathered for souvenirs. Among the injured men at the Pearl Harbor Naval Hospital:

"A great deal of interest was taken in the bits of shrapnel extracted from many of the wounds, and no sooner was the bit of metal out of some poor fellow than it was passed around from bed to bed, then carefully wrapped in tissue paper and stored away in the owner's bedside table."

Right: Sugar plantation executive Sam K. Toomey points out to radio announcer Ken Carney how American guns brought down a Japanese plane. The aircraft crashed in a sugar field and exploded; this tail section landed in a macadamia nut grove. *Below:* Pieces of shrapnel picked up at Hickam Field on Dec. 7th.

"I...found a two-inch wide hole in my yard. I dug down eighteen inches for the bullet. It happened to be one of our own American machine-gun bullets from Pearl Harbor."

Evacuation

E vacuation was a big topic early in the war. At first, *"...all of the women and children from Schofield and Wheeler Field were brought into town and taken to schools and churches, from where they were distributed to various homes...they sent...15 [to one home], six adults and nine children...However, they all returned to their homes on Thursday [Dec. 11]..."*

This was all small-time compared to what came next.

"...the military governor... immediately urged all non-essential civilians to leave."

This meant everyone whose job was not crucial to the war effort. The reason? Fewer mouths to feed, fewer people in the way should the Japanese return in force. Military dependents were forced by order to evacuate, but residents could stay or go. Those who departed were criticized, sometimes harshly:

"Are you not ashamed to leave now when it is your opportunity to do something...? ...How can you ever again face the friends you desert at a time like this?"

Sudden departures meant property had to be sold quickly and possessions left behind.

"Everyone is proud of...things inherited from people who leave. Thought I had a car

for awhile, but the Navy decided to ship it. But my friend...[did leave me] her canary..."

Most local people decided to stay.

"I am beginning to think only a coward would leave Hawaii...if we die protecting our home, OK. At least no one can say we didn't try."

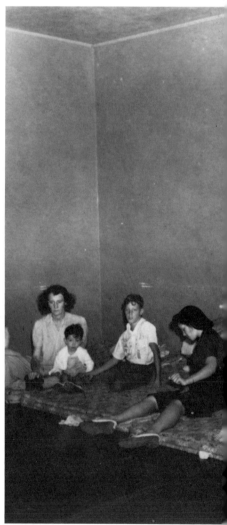

Above: Christmas Eve, 1941: With vacations cut short by war, tourists crowd the Matson Navigation counter at the Castle & Cooke building to register to leave Hawaii. Their return voyage in a military-controlled ship would be far less luxurious than the trip over had been. *Right:* Military wives and children spend the night of December 7th in temporary quarters. *Far right:* While awaiting evacuation to the mainland, *"These Army wives take no chances on losing their curves, war or no war"*- (original caption.)

"There are certain people who have to leave whether they want to or not...yet I know of...[others]...who are most anxious to get away..."

"Remember Pearl Harbor!"

A goodly number of Americans had had no idea exactly where the Hawaiian Islands were - much less Pearl Harbor itself - but they soon knew. And the slogan that reminded them of why they were fighting was part of a tradition that dated back to the 1800s. "Remember the Maine!" had been the most recent example; it commemorated a U.S. Navy ship which had been sunk in Havana harbor in 1898, an incident which had sparked the Spanish-American War.

Slightly less well-known, but in a similar vein, was "Praise The Lord and Pass The Ammunition." This phrase was spoken by Chaplain Howell Forgy of the USS New Orleans as he and other men sweated to pass antiaircraft shells to their ship's gun deck during the attack. Often printed and spoken during the war, there was even a song by this title.

"Remember Pearl Harbor!" served its duty as an instant rallying cry for all-out war effort. Naturally, a flood of patriotic memorabilia made use of the popular statement. Who can say whether this was all for a noble purpose...or just to earn a fast buck?

Remember Pearl Harbor

By

JOHNNY NOBLE

MILLER MUSIC, INC.
1629 BROADWAY · NEW YORK

Composed by
JOHNNY NOBLE

VICTOR

For best results use
RCA Victor Needles

27738-A

REMEMBER PEARL HARBOR—March

(Don Reid–Sammy Kaye)

Swing and Sway with Sammy Kaye

Vocal refrain by Glee Club

"The President of the United States immediately denounced [the attack] as treachery of the worst order...And now the slogan has spread to the farthest corners of the United States: 'Remember Pearl Harbor.' The American people will never forget, and they'll never quit until the attack has been fully avenged."

A variety of items carry World War II's most famous slogan. *Facing page, top:* This paper sticker could add a patriotic note to luggage (or any other surface). *Facing page, below:* A jewelry company offers a special "Lapel Pin" in a newspaper advertisement from April 1942. *This page, above:* Sheet music and a record label show how the phrase was used musically. (Although the titles are the same, these are actually two different songs. The version on the record was the more popular.) *Right:* A red, white, and blue plastic brooch forms a visual pun with the word "Pearl" replaced by an imitation pearl.

Getting Defensive

There seemed to be no question but that the Japanese would be attacking again. And when they returned it might not be just a hit and run raid - this time it could be an attempt to actually occupy the islands. All-out defense preparations were necessary, and fast. There weren't enough soldiers to do everything in the first few months, so thousands of civilians pitched in to help clear land and unroll barbed wire.

Meanwhile, the Bishop Museum and Honolulu Academy of Arts moved irreplaceable items to the safest places they could, and microfilm copies of important records at banks and the Territorial Archives were sent to the mainland. Some individuals even buried their valuables in the ground.

Facing page: The Hilo Minutemen (a volunteer civilian group) string barbed wire on a Big Island shore. *Left:* February 12, 1942: *"...the elaborate chandeliers which have hung in [Iolani] Palace all these years were dismantled and placed in storage until better days"* by Manuel Moreira and Joe Yamamoto of the Dept. of Public Works. *Below:* The war touches Waikiki - *"[Soldiers] have put barbed wire all along [the] beach...It seems so strange our once beautiful beach like this - But they left us a puka to go thru to swim -"*

Getting Defensive

Trenches

If bullets and shrapnel might soon be flying again, the best refuge would be underground. The easiest underground shelters to build, and the fastest, were trenches - so trenches there soon were, in most open areas. They were especially needed where people were concentrated, like schools. But these stopgap measures didn't meet with approval from everyone:

"[The trenches] are not deep enough. Why should one half of a person be protected while the other half is being shot away [?]"

"...you [find out] what it's like to huddle in a humiliating hole in the ground. You [realize]...that countless persons such as you, have had their lives snuffed out while they cowered there, unable to ward off the shrieking bombs and bullets."

Above: "We were asked to dig trenches at school one day. That was a military order...It was a back-breaking job, believe me." Parents and other volunteers go to work at Jefferson School in Waikiki. Students had to join in too at some schools.
Facing page: "...air raid practices were held. During these practices we crouched in ditches built along the school grounds." - a McKinley High School scene. *Left:* What happened to a good many trenches when it rained. With conditions like this, Hawaii was most fortunate its shelters were never put to real use.

57

Getting Defensive

Shelters

To protect Hawaii's civilians, an order from the military government early in the war demanded that every household construct its own shelter. These differed greatly: one in Kahala had "walls" made from an old ping-pong table covered with cheerful posters advertising a brand of cereal ("The delicious meal that keeps you fit!"), while a Diamond Head homeowner made use of an existing cement drainage pipe on his property. The landlord of a Makiki apartment house built one big shelter to hold all 24 of his tenants.

But all did not go smoothly. Many people lived in areas where the ground was too rocky to dig in, or where the sandy soil just wouldn't hold up. Some (especially small children) found that the dark holes were just too scary to go into, air raid or no. And everyone had a problem when it rained:

"...just before the air raid sounded last Sunday morning after a heavy rain we discovered [our shelter] had caved in along with many others in the neighborhood."

On a grander scale, over 1,000 public shelters (to be built by the government) were planned for Honolulu, but probably not more than 250 were ever built in parks and other open areas.

Below: Typical "splinter-proof" shelters, not actually strong enough to withstand a direct bomb hit, fill the park at Punahou Street and Wilder Avenue. (Note the sign on the utility pole.) *Facing page:* Edean Ross poses both outside and inside a shelter on the grounds of Iolani Palace in March 1942. Made to hold 50, experience showed that 85 people could fit. Oahu had 9 air raid alerts during the war, but during one of them, *"very few people were in the trenches or emergency shelters. Most stayed in their homes, or out under trees."*

"What are all these...long, earth-covered mounds, with open doors and steps leading to subterranean twilight? Bomb shelters!...Forceful reminder: We are at war."

Getting Defensive

Camouflage

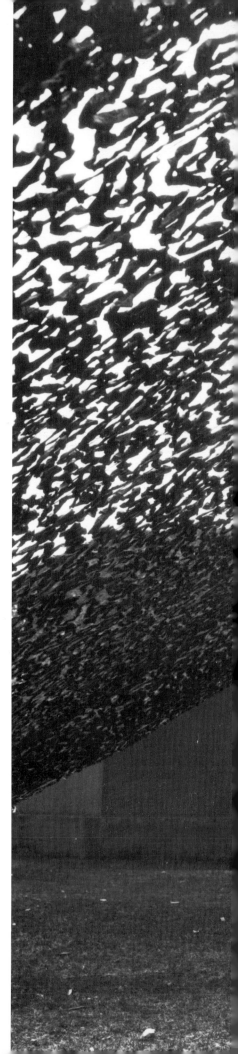

War brought a new art to the islands. *"Everywhere in Hawaii you see it nowadays - camouflage. Mysterious shadows surrounding certain areas. Variegated colors...smeared on buildings here, there, and yonder."*

Lei makers had an important role in this field:

"With the restricted and secret sailings and arrivals of ships, lei selling... ceased...But the army found a solution. Those same nimble fingers...are now engaged in making [camouflage] nets..."

This locally-made netting looked like vegetation and was draped on smaller structures to hide sharp outlines, while crucially valuable buildings like the headquarters of the Mutual Telephone Company were splashed with the familiar camouflage paint job. Theoretically, this would even make such things as Aloha Tower not so readily visible, but not everyone was convinced:

"...saw how the engineers had camouflaged all the big buildings - some atrocious & some very clever - tho some maintain that camouflage has no real value except to keep the people amused..."

Left: Fort DeRussy, January 1942: Capt. Trick, U.S. Engineer, inspects the work of lei maker Blanche Porter. Next, the strips of fabric woven into this camouflage net will be dyed in browns and greens. *Facing page:* The same type of netting on duty at Pearl Harbor. *Below:* Freeform patterns adorn the exterior of Hawaiian Electric's main downtown power plant.

The Enemy Returns

Above: Soldiers examine a crater left by a Japanese bomb at Tantalus. Many people wrongly believed that these bombs had been accidentally dropped by an American plane. *Left:* Yes, it's real money; the back of this $10 bill clearly shows the distinctive HAWAII overprint. With few exceptions, this was the only type of money anyone could legally use in the islands from July 1942 through October 1944.

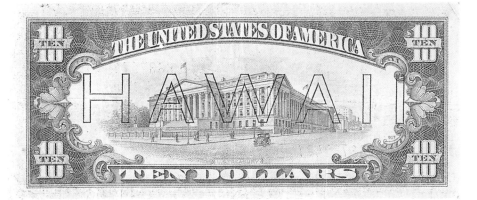

Hawaii's greatest fear was the very real possibility of the enemy attacking again.

The Japanese really did come back, but fortunately not in the numbers that they might have. Enemy submarines patrolled around the islands throughout December 1941 and January 1942, sinking at least six ships and even shelling Hilo, Kahului, and Nawiliwili harbors. In all cases the damages from these offshore sub attacks were minor.

Also minor - by sheer chance - was the damage in Honolulu from a Japanese bombing raid about 2 am on March 4, 1942. Two amphibious planes, launched from a submarine, flew a reconnaisance mission over Oahu that night. Because of thick clouds, the bombs they dropped never came close to the intended target of Pearl Harbor. The first load fell offshore while the second crashed into the slopes of Tantalus above Roosevelt High School, awakening thousands of city dwellers. The size of the resulting craters showed how much damage might have occurred had the bombs landed in an inhabited area.

If Japan had succeeded in occupying Hawaii, it could have wreaked havoc on the United States and the rest of the world by manipulating the supply of the islands' captured American currency. To forestall this potential catastrophe, all paper money in the islands was replaced by special bills bearing overprints that read HAWAII. Once collected, the $200 million in old money was burned, first in Oahu Cemetery's crematorium, and then in a sugar plantation furnace.

"...we were awakened by a terrible explosion and the smell of gunpowder...the Japanese dropped four bombs just a few yards away...it is impossible to describe the terrible loudness..."

Below: These barracks were built in Palolo Valley to house possible civilian evacuees in the event of a Japanese invasion.

EVACUATION INSTRUCTION CARD—DISTRICT A

(SEE MAP ON BACK OF CARD)

1. AN AIR-RAID ALARM IS NOT AN EVACUATION ORDER. Do not leave your home at an air-raid alarm. Just seek shelter in your splinter trench.

2. AN EVACUATION ORDER WILL BE ISSUED BY THE MILITARY GOVERNOR WHEN HE THINKS IT NECESSARY.

3. Take this card and map with you if you evacuate your home.

4. It is hoped that evacuation will take place during daylight hours, in an orderly manner, with sufficient time to enable all necessary arrangements.

5. All women and children (except boys over 15) will be advised (not compelled) to evacuate if they live makai the red line, and go to safer areas mauka.

6. Evacuees may make their own arrangements in advance of the evacuation order and move if they wish into safer areas. Anyone changing address will notify the Registration Office at Kaahumanu School. Enemy aliens must secure permission to move, from the Police Department.

7. Evacuees will be directed to a billet if they have not made previous arrangements with friends or relatives in safer areas, to whom they may go.

8. Upon leaving home each evacuee will take along an evacuation kit containing the following:

   2 blankets; 4 days' supply of food, preferably canned or cooked; change of clothing; toilet articles including soap, towel and toilet paper; medicines as needed; waterproof coat or other waterproof covering; flashlight; can-opener, gas mask, cup, plate, knife, fork, and spoon. Be prepared to pay a reasonable charge for your accommodations to the person who cares for you. Credit will be allowed for your food, if used.

9. Evacuees may go in automobiles, but no automobile will be allowed to leave the precinct unless filled to capacity. Or evacuees may walk to the assembly point. Serviceable shoes for protection against broken glass, etc., are desirable.

10. Men and boys over 15 are required by order of the Military Governor to remain in their precincts to help fight fires, etc. Women and girls employed at work that must go on, may remain in their homes or places of work.

11. Evacuation procedures are directed by the Evacuation Committee, under the supervision of the Provost Marshal.

12. It is hoped that an evacuation period will last only a short time, probably a few days, after which evacuees may return to their homes when notified by the Military Governor. Ask your Warden for needed information and further details. During evacuation, call the Evacuation Center where you first reported, for necessary information.

FRANK E. MIDKIFF, Chairman
Evacuation Committee

March 1, 1942.

FILL OUT IN DUPLICATE

NAME_____ ADDRESS_____

CHILDREN, with ages (except boys over 15)_____

_____

BILLET DESIRED_____ ADDRESS_____

Evacuation Plans

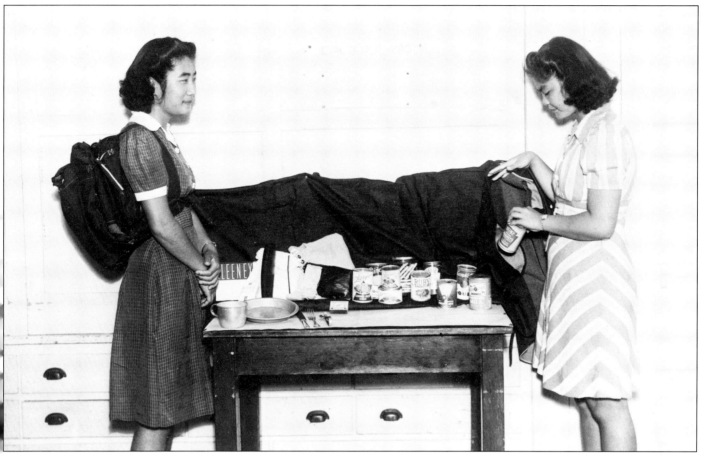

Facing page: Five official maps of Honolulu showed evacuation areas and billeting centers. Shown here is the back of one, with a list of proper actions to take and the contents of evacuation kits. *Above:* Two students from a Waialua High School home economics class demonstrate how $2.50 worth of denim fabric could be made into an evacuation kit.

The Office of Civilian Defense had a plan to deal with the nightmare of a possible Japanese invasion of Honolulu.

An east-west line was drawn about halfway through the city to divide it into two zones. Women and children makai of this line would have to move inland if the situation became desperate. Seventy percent of these potential evacuees planned to stay with friends or relatives in the "safe" area, and two large refugee camps were built in Palolo and Kalihi Valleys for those who had nowhere else to go. Published lists told what to carry in the required evacuation kits which each person was supposed to have ready at all times, and store windows even displayed samples to put the idea across. In addition to the canned food, blankets, and flashlight the kit had to have, some people packed valuables as well. One woman prepared a suitcase containing the family silverware, only to find she couldn't even lift it when it was closed.

The threat of invasion realistically only lasted for about six months. The Battle of Midway in early June 1942 effectively put a stop to Japanese expansion in the Pacific, and the islands could breathe much easier. Actually, although plans for the invasion of Hawaii certainly existed in Japan, they remained mostly theoretical. Fortunately, the great distances involved precluded a real occupation.

Rumor Capital, U.S.A.

Above: Members of the Junior Chamber of Commerce of Hilo placed these clever signs around their city at spots appropriate to each message; March 1942.

"When one looks back...and studies some of the stories that got around about this and that, one wonders about the credibility of humans."

I t goes without saying that during the days...following the attack...the air was filled to suffocation with all sorts of rumors."

Not only just following the attack, but indeed during the entire war years, people constantly repeated more rumors (both plausible and preposterous) than could ever be listed. Hawaii certainly wasn't alone in this tendency, for rumors were worldwide, and they spread vigorously in spite of efforts to stop them.

In the islands, the surprise attack shook people so thoroughly that every scrap of information was immediately seized, repeated, and embellished. Such as: enemy parachutists were landing and armed troops were coming ashore (they weren't). The Japanese fleet was still nearby (it wasn't). The water supply had been poisoned; men were signalling with lights to offshore ships; military leaders had not responded to the first word of the attack because they were playing golf or they were too hungover from parties the night before...and so on.

Among Hawaii's Japanese residents were thought to be numerous spies and saboteurs. Such tales were widespread; a 1942 Hollywood film, *Air Force,* showed snipers on Maui firing on a fictional American plane after it made an emergency landing there on Dec. 7th, and had an actor claiming that a group of "vegetable trucks" had driven past a line of parked aircraft on Oahu to smash the tail off each one during the attack. In real life, one woman feared for her life because *"...we had had stories as far back as 1940 & all thru 1941 that the [local] Japs...were all set to kill or poison every haole in the islands the moment war struck..."*

The most widespread rumor of all: island Japanese knew of the impending attack before it occurred. Considering the level of crucial secrecy around this most startling military event, it's absurd that numbers of civilians in the opposing country would be informed in advance.

Rumors subsided a bit (but didn't die out) as the war progressed. For example, someone would periodically come up with a date on which the Japanese would supposedly attack again (April 15, 1942 was one of them); and later on, as American troops flooded into Hawaii, stories circulated of rapes and other crimes said to have been committed by drunken military men. One man's diary listed these stories:

"...Three soldiers dragged a woman from her car at Aiea...What the newspapers do not print is what counts. Someday the real truth will come out...I heard: a few Marines entered the Lihue Hospital...and ordered all the Japanese patients out of bed. This done...the Marines got into the beds and went to sleep. I hope this isn't true!"

An especially popular tale from the summer of 1944 told of a mainland woman, either a nurse or a WAC, who was supposed to have remarked on a crowded Honolulu bus that where she came from, "the colored people give their seats to the white people." The Hawaiian girl this statement was loudly directed at then got up and slapped the woman in the face. Did it really happen? No!

Rumors were considered bad for morale at best, and dangerous at worst. The government fought them constantly. People could - and did - get in trouble for spreading them.

"We must not talk...I repeated a bit of news about an impending gas attack...An FBI agent tracked me down and checked up on me...I am afraid to even write down what I heard."

But rumors lived on just the same.

Above: This innocuous ad appeared in Honolulu newspapers a few days before the Dec. 7th attack and was later claimed to be some sort of warning. Among the numerous "hidden messages:" "by the Yard" referred to the Pearl Harbor Navy Yard, "Parade" meant "air raid" (if you dropped the P), the black design in the upper left corner looked like a cloud of smoke, and so on. This foolishness inspired a 1942 mystery novel entitled "Murder By The Yard," in which an innocent shopper checking out these advertised bargains finds herself kidnapped by a spy ring!

"[A particular building] appeared to be the only place available to set up a Headquarters...[so it] was requisitioned and occupied by the American Rule of 'take it and argue it out afterwards.'"

Above: One of a number of temporary buildings stretches across the lawn of Iolani Palace, indicating the presence of Hawaii's military government.
Facing page: This mass of paperwork represents the profusion of new agencies Hawaii had to deal with.

The Military Takes Over

In wartime, the United States government moved into civilian affairs to an unprecedented level, but nowhere in the country did this occur to the degree that it did in Hawaii. Here arose a unique situation never seen before, or since: the takeover and entrenchment of a military government, with the consequent loss of very basic American freedoms.

It all started on December 7th. On the afternoon of that tumultuous day, Governor Joseph Poindexter signed a statement prepared by the Army which turned over many of the functions of the civilian government to the military. This action distressed Gov. Poindexter greatly, but he did it because of the strong threat of further attacks by the Japanese. Lt. General Walter Short, who then announced himself to be the "Military Governor" of Hawaii,

reassured Gov. Poindexter that, if there was no danger of enemy landings, martial law would be lifted "within a reasonably short time." In fact, this was not to be the case.

Hawaii's government was then tremendously revamped. There were scores of new agencies, hundreds of new regulations, and an annoying lack of coordination among branches of the hierarchy that left many people unsure of just who was supposed to do what. With this new authority came huge changes; what the military needed, it could - and did - take. About half of the public parks in Honolulu changed over to storage depots or sites of military structures. Dozens of schools, both public and private, were seized, and much of what was in them had to be moved out with only a day or two's notice. (Most prominent of these takeovers was that of

Punahou School's huge campus at 1:10 A.M. on Dec. 8th by the Corps of Engineers. They stayed for the duration of the war.) Sugar and pineapple plantations found themselves giving up land, equipment, and manpower: Waimanalo Plantation turned 100% of its employees and facilities over to the Army for a full month after the attack. In the end, over 300,000 acres of land were occupied by the Army, Navy, and Marine Corps; the Army alone controlled a full third of Oahu! Some of this land was condemned and then paid for, but most was leased - although usually leases weren't signed until months after the property had been taken. Not all civilians accepted this happily.

The Military Takes Over

Martial Law

I haven't heard a single complaint concerning the military rule, for people just know that it's for their own best interest."

The stunning shock of war's arrival was enough to convince most citizens - at first - that strict and swift military justice was the best thing to keep slackers and saboteurs from causing trouble.

Civilian courts stopped functioning and everyone who committed a crime went before a military judge. *"Only the formal outline of the usual ponderous processes of peacetime justice remained"* as the judge listened briefly and then made his decision - which was utterly final unless a pardon was granted by the military governor. There was no possiblity of an appeal to a higher court because there no longer *were* any such courts. Lawyers were discouraged from being present. Furthermore, *"Justice cannot wait now, under martial law, for the formality of a search warrant," [a judge]*

said. *"We don't have time."* And in the most fundamental omission of all, a person could be arrested and held indefinitely without bail and without being informed of the charges against him.

Some people began to question whether this entire system was legal, and one crusading lawyer, J. Garner Anthony, brought the subject out in the open in May 1942. From then on there was a complicated battle to restore civilian law. Most of those who opposed the military were Democrats and labor unions; Republicans and bigger businessmen supported it. Some in the latter group had a strange idea that civilians were not really fit to govern themselves, and that raising a fuss about the issue was counterproductive:

"The military has a much too important job to do to be continually distracted by petty annoyances of court contests..."

But eventually such "petty annoyances" proved successful and martial law ended in

October 1944.

The final word came from the United States Supreme Court in 1946. Its ruling: military law as practiced in Hawaii had been unconstitutional.

"If I were asked, 'What was the worst experience I had all through this war,' my answer would be:'Martial Law!'"

"I am really tired of the kind of laws we have in Hawaii. I always thought we were fighting for freedom!"

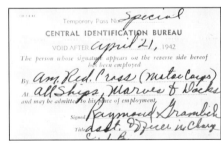

Facing page: Justice in wartime Hawaii: a military judge presides in court. *Above:* The Honolulu docks, formerly the scene of sentimental ship arrivals and departures, stand closed off to most civilians in evidence of military control. (Note camouflaged Aloha Tower.) *Right:* What you needed to get in - a pass.

The Military Takes Over

Blackout

Probably the regulation that affected life the most was the blackout. Rigidly enforced, there was no way around it; and it hit everyone right at home.

There had been some preparation. Practice blackouts were held in May of 1939, 1940, and 1941, with the latter two covering the entire Territory of Hawaii. U.S. planes had simulated an air attack during the 1940 event, and publicity handouts stated, *"Suppose this was in reality. You bet we'd BLACKOUT and in a hurry,"* and urged residents to *"do your part in this rehearsal for an event we hope will never come."*

But the event did come. When it did, islanders found out it was one thing to turn their lights off for 20 minutes or so in a test, and quite another to try to live a normal life in utter darkness with a sentry outside who was ready to shoot out any lights he saw - which really happened during those first few nights of war. A man standing watch outside Kapiolani Hospital in Honolulu had this experience:

"...the light attracted the attention of a roving patrol of 3 soldiers in a side car motorcycle, and armed with automatic rifles. They expressed the intention of shooting out the lights...not knowing the place was a hospital. We dissuaded them...that was the only worthwhile thing I accomplished during and following the Battle of Pearl Harbor."

Most folks simply didn't have the materials to do the job properly at first, so the only alternative was to just have no light at all.

"We are still talking about that first meal we attempted to eat in the blackest night of the blackout [Dec.7th]. We couldn't see each other nor anything on the table so we literally had to feel our way through the meal. If you reached out for something
you'd be liable to stick your finger in the butter or in somebody's eye."*

Optimists hoped that all this was just going to be for a short time.

"While we are strongly...for this blackout...we would feel a bit warmer in support of the idea if we felt it was a temporary arrangement, and not likely to run on into months, as someone has been skeptical enough to suggest!"

After awhile it became obvious that the situation *was* going to run on into months, so people carefully blacked out their homes by covering windows with tar paper or black paint. Then you could turn the lights on inside when the windows were shut, and no light could get out...but no *air* could get *in* either. There were no room air conditioners then, and people with electric fans were considered very lucky since these were soon impossible to get.

To insure a complete adherence to the rule, blackout wardens patrolled neighborhoods. This wasn't always easy:

"We are having a very exasperating time in our capacity as wardens for reporting lights in [Manoa] valley...Oh, the people were as exasperating as children in school," wrote one woman.

On the other hand, homeowners often found themselves at the mercy of nitpicking wardens who would report insignificant light leaks, such as keyholes.

"Which brings us to another gripe - those tickets for 'flash' violations...[the cops] camp on the curbs waiting for some absent-minded victim to show a momentary light - then nail him...That isn't intelligent policing - it's bullying the citizenry."

For even minor infractions of the blackout, people got hauled immediately to military court and sentenced: fines of hundreds of dollars and suspended jail sentences were
handed out for such things as the faint glow of gas stove burners or a lit cigarette being visible. Even the dim light of a radio dial was enough to bring on such punishment; it's fortunate that TV broadcasting did not yet exist!

Such a situation brought disapproval from the public, especially because the Honolulu docks and Pearl Harbor shipyard were not blacked out since work had to go on in these locations around the clock.

"...the welding arc from the Navy Yard...can be seen easily twenty-five miles away. And yet, the people of Hawaii live in total black-out!"

Gradually the restrictions were eased as the danger of bombing raids lessened. By July 1943, some lights were allowed to show outside homes, but *"the relaxation is experimental - and complete blackout will again be reinforced unless residents comply fully...Carelessness will be punished by reimposition of total blackout."*

Despite such threats, things only got better. Traffic signals began operating at night by September of that year, and by 1944 *"if you were lucky the street light went on again in front of your house...casting strange new shadows..."*

All blackout restrictions were removed, finally, in July 1944. No longer would anyone have to *"[sit] dismally in the dark."*

"We maintain blackout...and it is a real blackout, no half-way measures - no street lights, no electric signs, and no lights in homes that are visible from outside."

Tied in with *"the most rigid blackout in the world,"* Hawaii's military government also clamped its citizens under an extremely tight curfew. Without a pass, you simply could not be on the street after hours. If caught, you'd be arrested - or, at the beginning of the war, subject to the very real danger of being shot.

"The town was guarded by a voluntary home guard whose members had touchy trigger-fingers. All through the night shots would ring out. We did not wish to be...targets for American bullets. So we went to bed."

"I am not so much afraid of the Japanese as I am of our own armed forces. Boy! they'll shoot at anything."

As things settled down, there was some humor in the situation of such novice guards; a Kauai woman wrote of a man who called out, *"Halt and be reconditioned!"* instead of "recognized."

Humor aside, the curfew (whose hours were gradually reduced as the war continued) effectively brought almost all nighttime activities to a dead halt.

"...it is now about 6:30 p.m....[on] King Street...in the old days, one found thousands of people milling about at this hour. Now a ghost street. Shops securely battened...No bright lights. We are at war. Total blackout will be in effect in another hour."

Social activities were difficult.

*"Nowadays when a hostess wishes dinner guests she must invite them to spend the night..."*otherwise, the only other option was to *"just sit and listen to the radio and then go to bed."*

Why such extreme measures? Probably it was because Hawaii's ethnically-Japanese residents (considered suspicious) were simply too numerous to be moved wholesale into concentration camps, as on the mainland - and so severe restrictions

The Military Takes Over
Curfew

were clamped down on the entire population of the islands instead. Military Governor Lt. Gen. Delos Emmons loftily announced that *"people don't want to be out on the streets anyway"* and despite objections that the curfew eventually was unneeded, it stayed until July 1945. Freedom's return was happily received:

  "Curfew - may it rest in peace and smoulder into dust and have no resurrection!"

HONOLULU POLICE DEPARTMENT
HONOLULU, HAWAII
NIGHT PASS
GOOD ONLY _____ March 27 _____ 1945
Jaimie L. Cameron & Party , residing at
1303 O Center , is (are)
authorized to travel during the hours of Curfew to and from:_____
3066 Wailani Rd.

W. A. GABRIELSON
CHIEF OF POLICE

Center: This 1942 Chevrolet, although a military vehicle, shows the typical headlight coverings all cars had to have. *Upper left* and *Above:* On one nighttime drive, *"we were stopped by Police at three separate points, [and] had flashlights flashed on our faces as well as our* **special pass***..."*

"...the curfew hour is 10:00 P.M. but to drive at night one must have approved blackout lights which only faintly light the road..."

The Military Takes Over

I.D. Card Required

We've been chronicled, statisticked and fingerprinted...Our status, personal and economical, has been carefully detailed in black and white...This information was forced from us by two agent-esses of the law who descended upon us one bright morning...[and] we offered no resistance."

More evidence of the pervasive hand of the military on Hawaii was the requirement that everyone over the age of six years carry an identification card at all times. Before such cards could be issued, though, each citizen had to be counted and fingerprinted in what was the largest such project ever attempted anywhere in the United States. The legwork was done for the most part by schoolteachers who went door to door. (School was called off for weeks as they took care of this task.) Not everyone was cooperative, or for that matter could even speak English; one teacher had to resort to acting like a dog to find out from an aged Chinese woman if there were any pets in the household!

The initial intention of the I.D. cards was to insure that bodies could be identified in the case of bombing raids, but an additional benefit was that enemy saboteurs might be more easily singled out if they were able to sneak ashore. As usual in wartime Hawaii, being caught without your card meant arrest and a quick trip to the military provost court.

Many people, however, had to carry more than just this one government-issued card. Those whose jobs took them into military bases or other restricted areas, whether it might be to deliver supplies or fix telephones, needed cards or badges to enter these places as well. And not everyone could get one:

"To obtain [such] an identification badge...a detailed personal history must be made, which is thoroughly checked by military authorities."

Below: Newly-arrived mainland defense workers wait outside the I.D. card bureau in the basement of Kawaihao Church. *Right: Everyone* had to have a card, even First Lady Eleanor Roosevelt during her September 1943 visit.

"I looked over my identification cards today and boy!...If this keeps up I'll have to carry a suitcase around. My pockets just won't hold any more."

The Military Takes Over

Gas Masks

Across my left shoulder is a strap. *Hanging on my right is a gas mask attached to the strap. Yes, a gas mask. Never thought I would wear one...If the enemy attempts a gas attack on Hawaii, we must be ready for it."*

The use of poison gas had been an especially horrific part of the trench warfare of World War I in Europe. The Geneva Treaty had subsequently outlawed its use, but Japan was known to have violated this ruling in its war with China in the 1930s. So to be absolutely sure of protection for

Hawaii's civilians, the military very conscientiously issued a gas mask to everyone in the islands between January and March 1942.

These masks were understood to be only loaned to - not owned by - the individual, and they were to be carried everywhere, at all times.

"At first it was very exciting to have possession of a gas mask, but before long the weight of the object exceeded its novelty," and people began leaving the masks at home, or in other places too; by

June they were being lost at the rate of 12 per day, and by September about 3,000 were separated from their intended wearers. Those who cared enough could get a new one at a cost of $3.75. A rumor went around in February 1942 that persons found without their gas masks could be arrested and fined - actually a plausible claim at the time, but not true, and the following year one man wrote:

"I notice very few people carrying their gas masks. There is about one gas mask carrier to every one hundred who don't."

"I hope we never have a gas attack because if we do, brother! Your own mother wouldn't recognize you."

Facing page: Some adults (like these men) and most school kids were walked through clouds of tear gas to test masks for leaks and to show that they really worked. *Left* and *below:* Six Honolulu businessmen try their gas masks on for size.

The Military Takes Over

Gas Masks

After all the big folks got their gas masks, something had to be done for the little ones under the age of two. The solution was the locally designed and manufactured "bunny mask" - a cloth bag with decorative ears on top and a "window" made from used X-ray film that had been washed clean. (A different type was issued later in the war.) One mother dreaded the thought of how she'd cope with a gas attack:

"...all I'll have to do is to tell my six-year-old to don his mask, slip on mine...slide my year-and-a-half baby into her old type bunny mask, shoot the three-months-old into his, and pump [air into it] like mad. After all, what has an octopus got that a mother hasn't?"

Gas doesn't carry too far, so the effects of an attack would be localized. Instead of sirens, then, a series of 1,500 gas alarms made from old automobile brake drums were hung on utility poles and trees at intervals of 1,000 feet throughout Honolulu. Only emergency personnel were authorized to strike these crude gongs, and fortunately the only times they ever did so were during tests to see whether the alarms could be heard satisfactorily in their area.

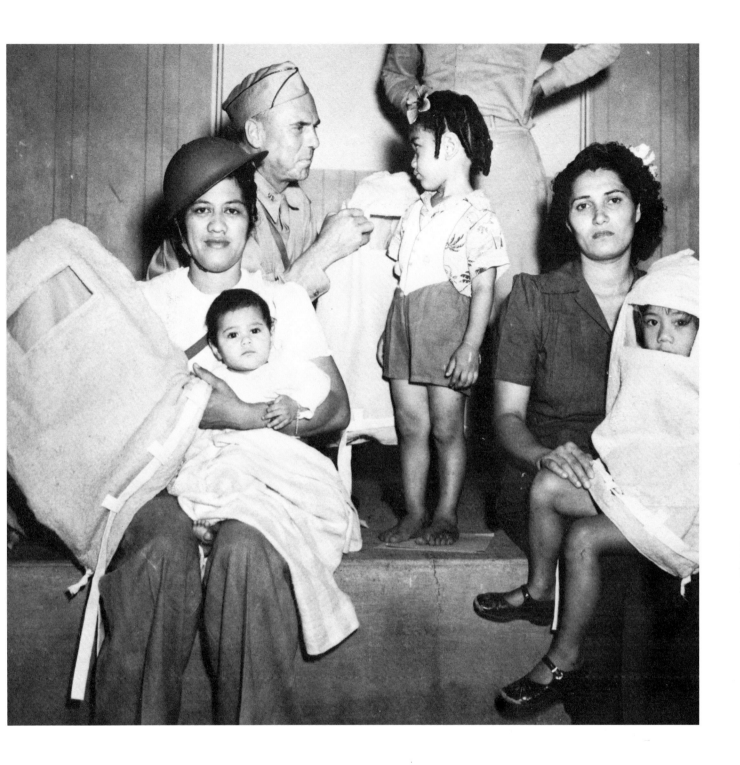

"What a mask! It seems the younger you are, the bigger the gas mask...Honestly, it's the most awkward looking outfit imaginable!"

Above: Little Barbara Jean Akau looks dubious as Col. George Unmacht prepares to envelope her in a bunny mask like Edith Mau (on the right) at Pohukaina School. *Facing page:* Marjorie Carter shows how a gas alarm would be sounded. Note the warning sign - the punishment for unauthorized use was a $500 fine or 6 months in prison, or both.

The Military Takes Over

Evacuate!

Just to be sure that it was possible, and to give emergency crews a chance to practice their roles, the Army staged its first grand evacuation drill of downtown Honolulu on November 4, 1943.

At 10:00 that morning, almost everyone inside a prearranged area in the very heart of downtown was ordered to leave. So shoppers, workers, and military personnel not on duty all streamed out, by car or in special busses or (in most cases) on foot. (No one panicked; they'd been warned that this was coming.) The thousands of evacuees then sat or milled around outside the deserted zone, on the ewa side of Nuuanu Stream or among the suburban homes on the slopes of Punchbowl, while regular traffic through downtown was rerouted.

Meanwhile emergency crews went to work. Policemen who had guided the evacuating hordes donned gas masks and watched as the Army set off smoke bombs and "simulated bomb bursts" which fire fighters then moved in to deal with. Imitation "casualties" played by military men stretched out on sidewalks awaiting discovery by air raid wardens and volunteer guardsmen. Overseeing all this was an Army cameraman who filmed the action from his position atop a small truck parked on Fort Street.

The emphasis in this drill - and in a similar one the following year - was on being safe rather than sorry. And fortunately, like so many of the other activities of the war years, the need to put all this practice into real action never arose.

Above: Evacuating crowds file past the Princess Theater on Fort Street, just mauka of Beretania Street. The appropriately-titled film lettered on the marquee ("Flight for Freedom") is a dramatization of the life of famous aviatrix Amelia Earhart..

More scenes from downtown's practice evacuation; November 4, 1943. *Above:* A fire truck will soon arrive to extinguish this smoke bomb at the intersection of Fort and Hotel Streets. Note that the policeman in the middle of the street, at left, is wearing his gas mask. *Left:* Two "casualties" are attended to on the King Street sidewalk of the Oahu Market.

The Military Takes Over

No Secrets from the Censor

Left: "This is the Royal Hawaiian Hotel and a part of the publicized Waikiki Beach,"was this postcard's original message. The movement of large numbers of men to the islands by the military was always secret, so the writer couldn't be allowed to say where the Army had sent him.

No one has much aloha for censorship. It is accepted - rather gracelessly in some cases - as one of the evils of war." The censors went to work right away on December 7th, and within days restrictions were put on newspapers, magazines, and radio broadcasts. The public, knowing this, gained a certain amount of skepticism about what they were being told:

"I know better than to believe everything I read in the daily papers. We would be fortunate indeed to sink three-fourths of the ships the newspapers and radios claim we did."

More immediate on a personal level was the censoring of all long distance telephone calls and all mail that left the islands. In the case of the former, a daunting set of restrictions had to be followed, and all calls had to be in English so the eavesdropping censor would be sure to understand everything. Among the many forbidden telephone topics: the weather. This was taboo for everybody; newspapers had to stop publishing weather forecasts since they might conceivably help the enemy to plan an attack.

Mail censorship was slightly less strict. Unacceptable information would either be inked out or cut out; if this wasn't possible, the letter would be returned to the sender to be rewritten. The objective was always to prevent important military-related facts from leaving Hawaii in case a ship might be sunk and its mail recovered by the Japanese. Also targeted: *"fantastic rumors obviously untrue and considered harmful."*

Mail censorship was not popular.

"I think most of us have deplored that more than anything else, because it is so extremely un-American."

Those who did this job for a living found it had its problems:

"We were not allowed to tell where we worked...At first, working at the censors was very interesting...[but] reading terrible letters day after day was quite upsetting..." and eventually boring, even for people who liked the idea of being able to snoop in the lives of others.

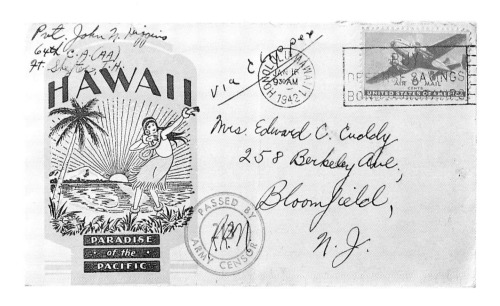

Above: Navy censors at work going over Christmas mail, 1943. Civilian censorship was a separate, non-military office for most of the war. **Right:** *"[The war] was a lot of little things...Remembering to write the return address far enough away from the edge of the envelope to allow the censor's seal..."* The Army censor's stamp is a serious contrast to the lighthearted hula girl design on this GI's letter.

Hurry Up And Wait

"We live from day to day...most of that time is spent standing in line for something..."

Hawaii lines up to wait out the war. *Above:* Just *part* of the line to get gas masks at Farrington High School in Kalihi on January 28, 1942. *Far left:* Pearl Harbor workers wait to purchase War Bonds on the first anniversary of the Japanese attack. *Left:* Shipments of mainland liquor took weeks to arrive; when they did, this was the familiar result.

A memorable feature of the war years were the seemingly interminable lines that everyone had to wait in. Either there wasn't enough of something to go around, or there were too many people, or both - but regardless of the reason, the lines were there. In the beginning, for example, you had to *"line-up to be fingerprinted... line-up for immunization against smallpox and typhoid...line-up for gas masks, gasoline coupons, liquor permits!"* (The waits for the latter ranged from 2 to 9 hours on the first day of issuance: March 1, 1942.)

After that, there were lines for all kinds of other things:

"...show lines extend around blocks, restaurants are flooded with the hungry...A person has to wait about twenty minutes in downtown Honolulu cafes for lunch."

A meat shortage late in the war produced the usual problem:

"[you] may have to stand in line for hours and yet not have [any] meat."

But there was nothing to do except grin and bear it.

A Ration-al Situation

F I

Five **Islands**

COMPOUND

DRY GIN

90 PROOF

CONTENTS: ONE QUART

100% FRUIT NEUTRAL SPIRITS

PRODUCED AND BOTTLED BY
BEVERAGE PRODUCTS
HONOLULU, T. H.

NOTICE: Re-use of this bottle for rectified spirits has been authorized as an EMERGENCY WAR MEASURE to conserve shipping space. The contents of this bottle are offered for sale ONLY as represented by this label, and only in Hawaii, for use in Hawaii. Any name, or other marking on the glass of this bottle is to be disregarded, since it has no relation to contents.

BEVERAGE PRODUCTS
HONOLULU, T. H.

Above: The company that made Five Islands products had to utilise various types of used bottles, since new ones couldn't be had...thus the notice on the bottom of the label. This locally brewed concoction was intended to take the place of scarce mainland liquor.

Most of the U.S.A. had to deal with the rationing of numerous necessities of everyday life, from sugar to shoes; but in the islands the only things rationed were gasoline and liquor.

Gas rationing took different forms in each of Hawaii's four counties in the first years of the war, but by 1944 the "ABC"system used on the mainland became standard. This meant that a vehicle would be classified according to its use and a lettered sticker attached to its windshield, with "A" designating the lowest monthly allotment. After that, the driver would always have to turn in a certain amount of ration stamps every time he bought gas.

"Liquor is rationed according to permits which...allow the bearer to buy one quart of hard liquor, one case of beer, or a gallon of wine a week. However, shipments are few and far between...[so] people are consoled with the local variety of gin...which is inclined to be rather rugged..."

Hawaii's supply of some scarce items (like butter) was greater than in other parts of the country; but in spite of the absence of outright rationing, there were still aggravating shortages of all kinds.

"...a bit of garlic or a few dry onions [are] something to be cherished. As to oranges...If I saw a piece of orange rind, I would look at it in amazement."

"In Honolulu fish in any size is worth its weight in gold."

"I wonder what a fresh egg tastes like."

And food was not the only problem:

"...one of the hardest things to buy in this town is a fountain pen."

"...at the shoe stores...'one pair per purchase...'"

Even if you were able to find what you were looking for, you faced competition from hundreds of others.

"Stores are cleaned out shortly after the merchandise arrives...An efficient shopper has to use the slogan, 'See it - want it - buy it - immediately.'" The result of all this:

"The rows of empty counters at Kress in their long white shrouds..."

Above: Gas rationing in the islands - the coupons were used first, on Oahu, and were good for 5 gallons apiece, 2 per month. Replacing such county procedures was the booklet below, standard throughout the country, which holds stamps in quantities according to a car's letter rating.

Right: Each and every alcohol purchase was to be notated on the back of this local liquor ration permit.

OFFICE OF DIRECTOR OF LIQUOR CONTROL   N⁰ 470216

PURCHASE PERMIT

Name ....

Street and No. ....

City or Town ....

Place of Employment ....

T. of H. Identification Certificate Sr. No. ....

Signature ....

To be filled in by Issuing Office

This PURCHASE PERMIT is granted to the person named herein in accordance with the provisions of Rule No. 55 prescribed March 9, 1943, by the Governor of Hawaii under the Hawaii Defense Act.

The receipt of the fee of $.50 is hereby acknowledged.

FOR THE DIRECTOR OF LIQUOR CONTROL:

LIQUOR COMMISSION OF:

Initials of Issuing Clerk

This Purchase Permit is Not Transferable

Kids At War

Wartime brought changes to everyone, including children. Schools were closed immediately after December 7th and stayed that way for the next few weeks or months; some never reopened at all since the military took over the buildings for their own use. This meant thousands of pupils had to be shifted to different campuses.

For one adult, *"The sight of little children trudging to school with gas masks is one of the most poignant reminders of the horror of total war,"* and along with gas masks came bomb shelter drills and first aid lessons for intermediate and high school students. Then, too, there were helpful afterschool projects to carry out, like packing games and magazines to send to convalescent soldiers, or rolling bandages for the Red Cross. Boy and Girl Scouts in particular

assisted in many wartime duties; one Boy Scout remembered how searching for "unexploded bombs" and "victims" in an Army manuever in Waialua in 1942 was like *"an over-emphasized game of hide-and-seek."*

Facing page: The "Barefoot Army" of Ewa executes "present arms," led by "Corporal" Ernest Tamashiro; July 10, 1942. *Above:* Led by Mrs. Edith Chang, Liliuokalani School students Abigail Ching, Eva Castro, Lila Lee, and Richard Choy practice first aid on "victim" Johnson Wong in March 1942. Behind them, classmates crouch in a shelter trench.

"Our boys and girls, irrespective of race, color, or creed, are all Americans and each one loves the flag he proudly salutes!"

Kids At War
Child Labor

Left: Not only boys shined shoes; these girls worked on Kalakaua Avenue near the Ala Wai Canal, by Kau Kau Korner, in 1942. *Right:* The other street trade practiced by kids, seen here in 1945. *"Newsboys..are better organized and supervised..."* than the troublesome shoeshiners, but they could still be annoyingly pushy: *"It is...common to have a [boy] shove an open newspaper in one's face...standing directly in the path...of the prospective customer."*

W ar was a disruption of childhood for many. A severe shortage of manpower for agricultural work forced sugar and pineapple plantations to turn to the only other possible work force: kids. Starting in 1942 and continuing through the war years, boys and girls from about 8th grade up, and from public and private schools all over the islands, put in one day a week working in the fields.

"...we were practically drafted for the job..."

"...but we all joined because it was a chance to miss a day of school." Many of these new laborers thought at first that their jobs would be something like a big school picnic; instead they found that although sometimes *"it proved to be fun working all together"* still *"...at the end of the day, I feel as though I had worked for a full week...mud on and in my shoes, mud on my pants, mud on my face, mud all over me..."*

Students soon figured out that sugar cane was better to work in than pineapples, since you could hide in the rows of taller cane plants when you wanted a break! Some schools gave academic credit for the work, and everyone got paid - but not too much:

"At the end of the day my total earnings came to eighty cents. I had cultivated eight hundred feet of canefields..."

The major lesson they learned:

"Working in the cane fields made us realize how hard our parents worked."

There were plenty of other jobs that needed doing and high school seniors were urged to drop school in favor of work. Early in 1942, about 4,000 did so.

"Many are the chagrined fathers who have discovered that their young [son] is getting $1 an hour, whereas...papa had been slaving for the past 10 years at 75 cents an hour," and under such circumstances, it's obvious why some students never finished their schooling.

Not all young people were so productively employed.

"One of the strangest out-of-school businesses has sprung up. Hundreds of boys...roam the business area, carrying small boxes containing boot black supplies and a stool. They ply their trade of bootblacks as sidewalk merchants...[numbering] 1,200 and upwards."

These street kids were a problem:

"For molesting pedestrians and making nuisances of themselves, the shoe shine boys are probably the worst. Newspaper vendors, however, run them a close second. Along Hotel Street...shoe shine boys - apparent ages, 6 to 12 - grasp...at the hands or clothing of passersby, particularly service men...[and shout] 'Shine, Mac,' and 'Hi, Pal'..."

The Honolulu Board of Supervisors finally passed an ordinance in 1944 putting controls on the situation: age restrictions, putting certain areas off limits, and requiring the kids to have permits to work.

SALVAGE for VICTORY
[SA]VE YOUR WASTE PAPERS, OLD
RAGS. RUBBER. & SCRAP METAL
[COLLE]CTION DEPOTS AT 25 PUBLIC SCHOOLS ★

Above: A typical cheesecake pose beloved of '40s photographers: Floyd Fitzpatrick of the Junior Chamber of Commerce presents a $400 check to four USO showgirls. The donation was earned through the sale of scrap materials in July 1942. Recycling cardboard locally (like the load in the truck) saved shipping space for war materials.
Facing page: Kids at work for salvage: Boy Scouts roll old tires in to a Beretania Street service station; the "Girls' Victory Club," organized by Evelyn Reitow (2nd from left, front), collects scrap materials door to door (both June 1942); and Kapalama School students show off their salvaged aluminum.

Salvage for Uncle Sam

America's war industries demanded great quantities of materials, but some were hard to get - especially rubber, since the Japanese had cut off the U.S.A.'s supply from Asia. There was rubber available...but it was still in use, in various forms, all over the country. To procure it (and many other materials), the public was exhorted to turn in all they could for salvage.

The first big rubber drive took place from May to July, 1942. Children were especially motivated to help out:

"I never saw the kids work so hard...They are really serious about it..." said one man.

As the collection of bathing caps, slippers, shoe heels, sink stoppers, toys, and (mainly) old tires grew, a vacant Ala Moana lot became a mountain of rubber. One man donated a 7 foot long rubber gasket he'd removed from a captured Japanese mini-sub that had helped in the Pearl Harbor attack. Hawaii's final total was over one thousand tons.

In addition to rubber, different metals were needed too; aluminum was being collected even before Dec. 7th. A prominent victim of metal salvage efforts was the Phoenix Fountain in Kapiolani Park, erected in 1919. Commemorating the ascendency of the Emperor Taisho, it had been funded by the contribution of $1 apiece by each of Hawaii's Japanese households. The fountain was dismantled and recycled, bronze phoenix and all.

Victory Gardens

"Private vegetable gardens have become very popular...Some [plants] won't grow at all and there is a constant battle with bugs and worms but we manage..."

People can live well on vegetables - *Millions eat nothing else!...Get ready now; the best growing season is just around the corner and a food shortage may be around the same corner."*

So read a January 1942 magazine ad that urged the planting of home Victory Gardens to combat erratic and tight shipping. In Honolulu, there were 13 large community gardens in parks and vacant lots and an estimated 15,000 home gardens by August 1942. Helen Poindexter, daughter of the Governor, started one at Washington Place; for many people the dirt piled on top of their backyard air raid shelter was the best spot.

Facing page: Vegetables grow in front of impressive Central Union Church. **Left:** University of Hawaii President Gregg Sinclair (right) and Adm. Chester Nimitz (wearing a lei made of tiny vegetables) inspect carrots presented at a Victory Garden Show on Lei Day 1943. **Below:** A community garden in the park bounded by Paki and Leahi Avenues in Kapahulu; May 1942.

Dogs for Defense

"I n this total war in which not only you but your pet is to serve, your dog, no matter what its breed, age, or sex, may make a good soldier..."

Not only human beings fought the war - man's best friend was called on to help out. Early in 1942 a national organization called "Dogs for Defense" was formed with the purpose of assisting the military in finding and training dogs to play a role in the war effort. Locally, wealthy canine breeder Harold Castle spearheaded the drive:

"Dogs are volunteered to the service of their country on the same basis as a man in the regular Army. He or she, as in this case both sexes serve equally well, is offered by the owner...on the understanding that the dog will be returned to its home, if all goes well, at the end of the war..."

One of Castle's own dogs, "Quester," was the first animal to be used, as a guard for military governor Gen. Delos Emmons.

Although in theory any mutt might have a chance to "enlist," there were certain physical requirements that had to be met.

"...dogs must be of proper size...[and] of the right age, one to five years..." and some also had to be intelligent and bold enough to "be trained in attack work." Most would function as assistants to human guards on night duty.

About 900 of the 3,000 dogs who were offered were accepted and trained. Those that made it through the war were deprogrammed in a special kennel at Fort Armstrong before going home.

Above: A possible canine soldier-to-be at a mass recruitment gathering at Thomas Square; July 5, 1942. *Right:* Dog on duty: at Koko Head, a carrier pigeon is placed in a container strapped to "Sir." *"He will then carry the bird to a mountain outpost for the flight home;"* September 1943.

Wartime Wahines

abor shortages were acute through much of the war in Hawaii. With men off in the armed forces or working on defense projects, job vacancies were numerous - and women were heartily urged by the local government to fill them. In most cases these were in fields that were traditionally female:

"The [high school] graduate can be more or less 'choosy' about...employment...If the student's a girl, she has a wide range of office work to pick from..." but for the first time a number of women broke into areas where they'd never been before. As military workers they drove trucks, handled supplies, and repaired equipment. In the civilian world, stores, restaurants, laundries, and just about every other business was chronically short of employees, and women filled in there as well.

But often this was not easy. To begin with, all workers had to put in an extra four to eight hours a week (beyond the usual forty) and most holidays weren't observed. Then, of course, came the regular feminine chores of marketing and taking care of the kids, all made more difficult by wartime conditions. Many women no doubt thought that, in war, *"it's all work and no play in Hawaii."*

"Everybody works - there is not enough help to go around...even husky Hawaiian girls are now doing manual labor for good pay."

Facing page: A female welder at Pearl Harbor. *Below:* Street sweepers Annie Navarro, Mary Cheong, and Agnes Pimental pause in their work in Honolulu's civic center; Oct. 21, 1942. *Far below:* Anita Davis repairs airplane parts at the Hawaiian Air Depot in 1942.

Volunteers For Victory

Every citizen could see that war brought innumerable new duties that desperately had to be taken care of: defense projects needed completion, crops needed harvesting, lonely soldiers needed company, the police and firefighters needed extra assistance, and much more. Existing agencies couldn't take care of all these needs. Who would do this work? Mr. and Ms. Hawaii knew their help was required, and that they could not be paid for it. So, admirably, they volunteered.

At the start of the war, there were not yet enough military personnel in the islands to do all the necessary defense work, so civilians took over the tasks of placing barbed wire and clearing land of thorny kiawe trees; on Oahu and Kauai thousands of men did the latter job. It was considered dangerous to expose local Japanese men *"to the hazardous possibility of being mistaken for an enemy,"* so instead of guard duties that involved weapons, their work was to prepare campsites for possible evacuees. This *"meant that they would do considerable manual labor...all free for nothing."*

Not all volunteer work was as rugged. *"The women of the islands are doing their share...[in] Red Cross units...scores of women gather each day for the making of surgical dressings...Other groups of women are taking hospital training. Another group is handling USO activities..."* and one of these necessary USO jobs was that of hostess and dance partner at nightly dances.

More than 2,800 young women (the USO Junior Volunteers) did this, some as often as 3 or 4 nights a week. All those who managed to keep up steady volunteer positions like these, in addition to a regular job, certainly showed a praiseworthy dedication.

"I did my share of...rolling bandages, digging air raid shelters, [and] partaking in numerous service projects..."

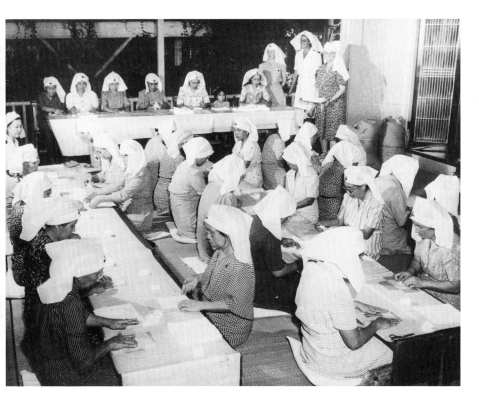

Facing page: Helping a sailor donate blood are Red Cross canteen worker Mrs. Zadoc Brown and Motor Corps worker Mrs. Thomas King; January 16, 1943. *Left:* To demonstrate their loyalty to the United States, Japanese women prepare bandages for the Red Cross. The nun-like head coverings they wear prevent loose hairs from ending up in with the gauze.

Volunteers for Victory

2nd Platoon
F Co Kauai Volunteers, 2nd Bn, Koloa, Kauai
Oct. 22, 1944

"We worked...to prepare our defenses...We volunteered for service as messengers, air raid wardens. We drove ambulances and studied first aid. We joined the Territorial Guard, the BMTC, the Police Reserve."

Probably the greatest numbers of volunteers worked for Civil Defense. One out of every 18 Oahu civilians was participating in these activities by May 1942; this was encouraged *"to not only give civilians something to do but to provide protection on a far greater scale than would otherwise be possible."*

Air raid wardens got to know their neighborhoods well on their nightly patrols, watching for blackout violations and ready for other possible troubles. Trained in firefighting and defense against poison gas, most wardens were men, but women joined up too. In 1942, nearly 30,000 volunteers in all took part; but enthusiasm lagged as the war progressed, and by late 1943 *"Of some 8,000 wardens...less than one-fourth [are] consistently active."*

One element of the Hawaiian war scene was unique in the entire country: the Organized Defense Volunteers, a group of nine different units of civilian men who functioned in a quasi-military capacity. These home guards numbered as many as 20,000 in all and were active on each island; they purchased their own uniforms but used weapons provided by the Army. Sentry duty was their usual task, but had Hawaii been invaded they would have been far more active. The Hawaii Rifles, Businessmens' Military Training Corps (BMTC), Maui Volunteers - and all the others - were often composed predominately of one racial group or another, either intentionally or by chance. As with other volunteer organizations their level of active participation decreased as the war went on.

Left: A civil defense armband. *Above:* The Kauai Volunteers were almost all Filipino plantation workers, anxious to have a role in the war effort since their homeland was occupied by Japan. *Right:* Military Governor Gen. Emmons and civilian Governor Poindexter (in hat) review the 5,000 steel-helmeted air raid wardens who attended a Civil Defense rally in Honolulu Stadium in May 1942. As the first such gathering in the nation, it was filmed for mainland newsreels.

Working In Wartime

The money that people are making at Pearl Harbor is almost unbelievable. No wonder every other person I meet is either working for the Navy or planning to work for them."

Both the Army and Navy needed innumerable civilian workers, particularly the latter at its Pearl Harbor shipyard. All these new high-paying jobs were such a strong lure that local industries lost employees steadily to the military, to the point where labor controls were put into effect and men were "frozen" at their existing jobs if they were deemed to be in an essential position. Even so, every local business had chronic staffing problems and finding good workers was difficult:

"...as one official told me...'a man that works two days each week, even though drunk, is much better that no man at all.'"

There were far more jobs available than there were local men to fill them, so thousands of mainland workers were brought to Hawaii. Lack of housing was the worst of the many problems this migration created. In some cases, war workers were forced into situations where as many as 18 men took turns sleeping in one room, in shifts. There was military-provided housing, but it was often far away from town, and most men worked such long hours they couldn't get shopping or banking done.

"...the war worker [is] Hawaii's unsung hero. A lonely man is he, far from his own home...Few comforts has he, and few pleasures after hours of grueling labor..."

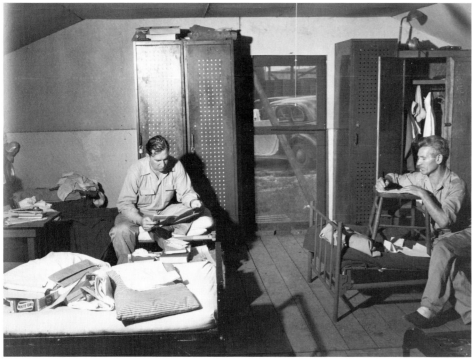

Facing page: This flag was sent to the kin of mainland war workers. Displayed in a home's front window, it was similar to the service flags that showed that a family member was in the armed forces. *Above:* "Messing Club No. 1" fed Pearl Harbor civilian workers. Such places served thousands during an 18 hour day. *Left:* Military housing for war workers was not too luxurious, but it was better than nothing; Fort Ruger, Honolulu, 1945.

Promoting Patriotism

The image on the sign reads:
"1 94 HAPCO EMPLOYEES LAID OFF TODAY.
THE PINEAPPLE THEY DIDN'T PACK HELPED
FEED THE AXIS, THANKS!"
HITLER - TOJO - MUSSOLINI

That good old American advertising know-how went to war just like everything else.

On one level, everyday newspaper and magazine ads were often entirely war-related. Similar in purpose, but on a much grander scale, were the campaigns that actively pushed patriotism. For example, the aim of the "Serve In Silence" drive was to reduce rumors and the spread of talk about military matters that might be overheard by enemy agents. ("Don't Be A Blaboteur!" shouted a poster in one store's display window.) Another, bigger campaign was the "Governor's Work To Win" crusade. Employers confronted with absenteeism and high turnover were the beneficiaries of this effort, which sought to convince people to stick to their jobs. The campaign utilised posters, a short film, and print advertisements that pictured workers of all types who were committed to help win the war by staying conscientiously on the job. A well thronged rally at Honolulu Stadium in May 1943 (the "Cavalcade To Victory") kicked off the whole affair, and featured such spectacles as a mixed group of military men and civilian workers wielding giant rifles to symbolically destroy caricatured figures of America's enemies. (Similar but less elaborate gatherings followed at other locations.) On its final and most personal level, the campaign awarded pins to individuals who had maintained perfect attendance records at their jobs for periods ranging from 2 months to 5 years. One recipient wrote proudly:

"This token of appreciation...is a morale builder if there ever was one...this Work to Win campaign is the flower of every other [campaign] yet attempted..."

Hawaii VICTORY WORKER

Far above: As part of the "Governor's Work To Win" campaign, the three enemy leaders of the Axis countries (Germany, Japan, and Italy) cynically congratulate Hawaiian Pineapple Company employees who missed work. *"The pineapple they didn't pack helped feed the Axis, thanks!"* (August 1943.) *Above*: A pin awarded for perfect job attendance in the same campaign. *Facing page:* Stores often featured war-related themes in their windows."*The Liberty House [was] first with a gas-masked mannequin window display"* in February 1942.

Buy War Bonds!

"Let your answer to bombs be BONDS!...Buy War Bonds and Stamps every day. Buy as if your very life depended on it. IT DOES!"

W ar Bonds were a way to get people to invest money with their government, for two reasons. First, the U.S.A. needed the funds to pay for the incredible amounts of war machinery that were being manufactured. And second, with the country more prosperous than it had been in years, just about everyone had cash - but there was very little to buy, since most industries were producing for defense. This could easily lead to inflation; to prevent that (by taking money out of free circulation,) citizens were constantly barraged with orders to BUY WAR BONDS!

There really was no escaping the sales pitch. You could buy bonds in banks, as you would expect, but they were for sale almost everywhere else too: at sporting events, in stores, at the Post Office, in theater lobbies, at special sidewalk booths, and even door to door. And if for some reason you still hadn't purchased a bond after encountering all this, you might receive one as a gift!

Holidays and special events became ways to promote bond sales with rallies held, for example, on Kamehameha Day. Captured enemy weapons were displayed to heighten interest; the lobby of downtown Honolulu's Bishop National Bank once held a Japanese Zero airplane.

Islanders responded to all this effort in an outstanding fashion. Local per capita bond purchases were the highest in the nation and in addition, Hawaii was the only state or territory in the whole country to consistently exceed the sales goal set by the government in each of the nine bond sales drives. A proud record!

Above: A Dairymen's Milk truck carries forth the word. *Left:* Standing ready for business at a special bond counter in the downtown Liberty House is Betty Pattison. On July 3, 1942, in the middle of "Retailers For Victory Week," half of Honolulu's merchants sold only War Bonds and no other merchandise during "Uncle Sam's Quarter Hour" from 11:45 to noon. *Facing page:* Lei seller Mrs. Lillian Kaahea happily holds $350 worth of War Bonds on Lei Day 1943, having heeded the advice to "Buy Uncle Sam A Lei of Dollars."

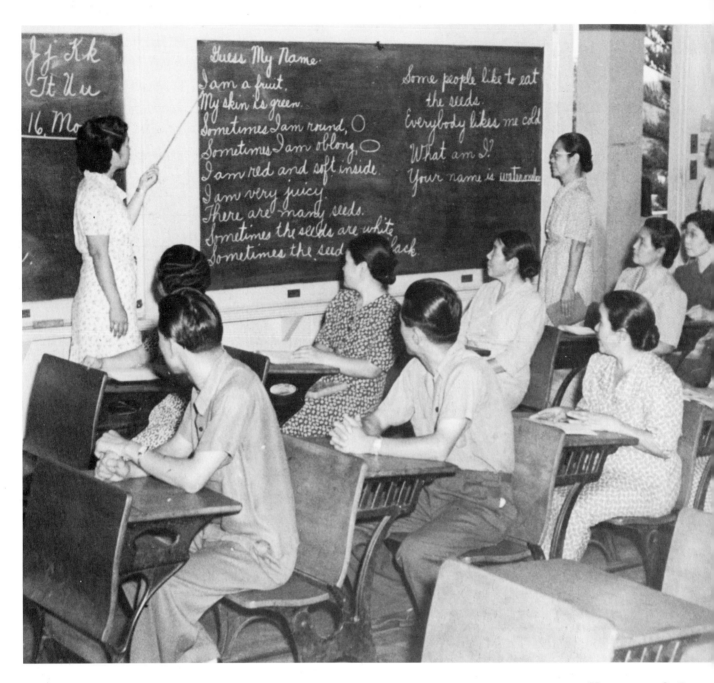

"Naturally we felt some suspicion of them."

The Japanese

Above: An adult English language class for Japanese speakers at the Kaimuki YMCA. *Above right:* Internee Charles Hasebe is interrogated with the assistance of interpreter Forrest Garnett (right) at Honolulu's Immigration Station; February 17, 1942. *Left:* The internment camp on Sand Island contained mostly Japanese, but about 50 Europeans were held also.

J
apanese planners and plotters have taken cold, scheming advantage of the tolerance of Americans. Japanese nationalistic institutions...have been [ways]...to conceal and carry forward the all-dominant plan of Japanese...conquest."

Japanese inhabitants of Hawaii faced a difficult and sometimes frightening period during the war. Suspicion and outright hatred were directed toward them.

"Many of the Japanese fear that they will be harshly treated...a younger Japanese woman said...'I am so ashamed. I do not like to have people look at me. I wish I could change my face."

Faces could not be changed, but names could: in 1942, 247 Japanese family names were legally changed, such as Kimura (to Kealoha) and Nakamura (to McFarlane.) More frequently, first names alone were Americanized; 2,400 such switches were made during the war years. And as they shed their names, many people threw out or burned ethnically Japanese objects and even family records. All of Japanese culture, it seemed, had been tainted, including the language.

"Many among us still speak, almost

exclusively... Japanese...So long as any group persists in using the language of the enemy, it is inevitable that they will arouse the suspicion that they also think with the enemy. It is their duty...to SPEAK AMERICAN!"

Those Japanese (mostly aliens) who were considered possible security risks were picked up starting within hours of the attack. Eventually, about 1,441 local Japanese were interned; 980 of them for the duration of the war. Many of these were sent to the mainland for their imprisonment. Although there was discussion of doing the same to all island Japanese, it was realized that, at the least, the logistics of moving 150,000 people made this impossible. Thus, fortunately, the Japanese of Hawaii escaped the wholesale internments of the rest of the country.

The Right To Fight

I *wanted to be of service to my country. Since I was of Japanese ancestry, I was told not to show up for work at the Naval Hospital. I felt bitter and sullen, and thought to myself, if they...cannot trust me, an eighteen year old kid, things were really bad."*

Suspicion of the loyalty of young AJAs (Americans of Japanese Ancestry) initially was strong. A McKinley High School teacher wrote to his students:

"You might as well admit it now that you are on the spot...you can, you MUST, show considerably more enthusiasm for our [war] struggle..."

Events later proved that they and others like them showed enthusiasm in abundance.

Japanese men who wanted to enlist in the Army were not accepted at the start, but two groups changed this. First were the AJAs already in the National Guard, who were consolidated into the 100th Battalion. Second were the former members of the Territorial Guard, who had all been discharged a few weeks after the attack on the basis of their race. To prove themselves, some formed the Varsity Victory Volunteers - 150 young men who engaged in difficult manual labor for the Army.

Having thus demonstrated their willing trustworthiness, Japanese men were allowed to enter the service starting in January 1943. Of the 9,500 who volunteered, about 2,700 were accepted. After a huge send-off rally at Iolani Palace, they sailed for basic training on the mainland and eventual glory as the 442nd Regiment, the most decorated unit in the Army for their brilliant successes in Europe.

"...Hawaii owes a special debt of gratitude to the Americans of Japanese ancestry fighting in Europe..."

Facing page, above: AJA volunteers on Kauai gather for a cheer before having their Army physical. *Below.* More than 2,000 new inductees march down King Street to Iolani Palace for their farewell gathering; March 28, 1943. *This page, above:* Florence Shirotake gives a paper lei and a handshake to Lt. Robert Kadowaki at the Iolani Palace aloha rally.

115

THE MILITARY

Friendly Invasion

Previous pages: A solitary hula dancer finds an appreciative audience at the Army-Navy YMCA in downtown Honolulu.
Right: The 4th Marine Division is welcomed to Maui. Such lavish ceremonies were infrequent; this one was an exception that occurred near the end of the war.

Within 10 days [of Dec.7th] two fast convoys had left San Francisco loaded with men. And in the next three-and-a-half years men...came in a flood to begin building from Hawaii the road to Tokyo."

When those first men arrived in the islands just after the war's beginning they came to defend the Territory. But in less than a year the emphasis shifted to the offensive, and Hawaii soon became the funnel through which over a million troops eventually passed - all of them necessary for the intense battles that would take back the islands throughout the Pacific that Japan had seized.

For these men there would be little of the prewar Hawaiian glamor that they'd seen in advertisements or Hollywood movies. In most cases their arrivals were fairly secret, so they rarely received a real welcome.

Ships came and went and residents never knew just how many troops traveled through.

"A long time ago there was Harry Owens' band on the radio from the Royal Hawaiian...It would be a wonderful place to go sometime, we thought...So what the hell. We got there, didn't we?"

Below: A column of soldiers marches along Queen Street at the Honolulu waterfront just after disembarking in April 1942. They're heading for trucks to carry them to Schofield Barracks.

Friendly Invasion

"The population of the Territory has expanded amazingly...any casual observer on the streets of Honolulu...could see that uncounted thousands of soldiers and sailors have arrived..."

It is impossible to state exactly how many members of the military were in Hawaii during the war years. The numbers changed constantly, but it's safe to estimate that at times the amount of armed forces on Oahu (which hosted the brunt of the influx) certainly exceeded the total of civilians on the island. The result, needless to say, was human congestion at a level never before seen in Hawaii.

"I listen[ed] to a barrage of complaints concerning the evils of over-crowding in Honolulu. One couldn't get a decent meal, people cleaned out the stores like a swarm of locusts...there were just too damn many people on this damn rock, and something ought to be done."

Facing page: This typical jam-up on a Honolulu Rapid Transit Co. bus on King Street in 1945 is partly the fault of gas rationing. **Left:** *"Salespeople are busy...Five minutes go by, ten minutes, twenty. He flags down a passing salesgirl. 'Sorry sir,' she says, 'I'm the stock girl. I'm not allowed to wait on customers.'"* **Below:** Military pedestrians outnumber civilians at the Fort/King intersection in Honolulu in February 1945: *"...it is almost worth your life to get through the busy downtown streets."*

Building Boom

I was amazed...Out of nowhere it seemed, there had sprung up a city of red-stained, olive drab tents placed side by side and row after row..."

All those hundreds of thousands of soldiers, sailors, and marines pouring into Hawaii had to have places to train and to live. There were certainly not enough existing buildings to house them or the equipment they used; temporary structures had to be put up, and quickly.

To do this the armed forces took over huge areas of land, mostly on Oahu. By the end of the war the services owned or were using almost 400,000 of Hawaii's 4 million acres. Island residents watched in astonishment as former agricultural tracts and unoccupied lands were transformed within days.

"Buildings are coming up overnight. The U. S. Army is changing cane-fields into villages." The ugliness of what resulted was disturbing:

"The roadside was clogged with hundreds of men [near Schofield]...Rows and rows of drab tents, barracks, and quonset huts stretched to the horizon, which shimmered in heat and dust."

In addition to new buildings, the military took over and enlarged all 5 of the islands' larger airports and built major roads like Nimitz Highway on Oahu and the Big Island's Saddle Road. To list all the many camps and storage depots and training centers that appeared in Hawaii in those first years of the 1940s would take pages; suffice it to say that such a sudden, widespread construction program is not likely to ever be seen again.

Above left: The largest of the Big Island's military settlements: Camp Tarawa, home to 4,000 Marines, in the town of Kamuela; December 1944. **Above:** *"From the top of the Pali this vast stretch so neatly arranged looked like a toy city..."* Camp Pali, seen here in August 1945, was one of 50 Army bases on Oahu. **Right:** Two views taken less than one year apart from the same vantage point demonstrate the speed and tremendous scope of military construction. In April 1944, left, work had barely started on the Waipio Amphibious Base at Pearl Harbor. By March 1945, right, the bustling docks (built partly on landfill) were in full operation.

Training The Troops

Above: *"He is taught to be mean and especially how to kill men in the quietest possible way..."* At a Jungle Training School, an instructor shows how to capture or kill a man from behind; November 3, 1943. **Facing page, above:** The sign at the entrance to a joint Army/Marines training center at Schofield Barracks in 1943 says it all. **Right:** Two Maui residents watch from a beachside front yard as men take part in amphibious landing practices.

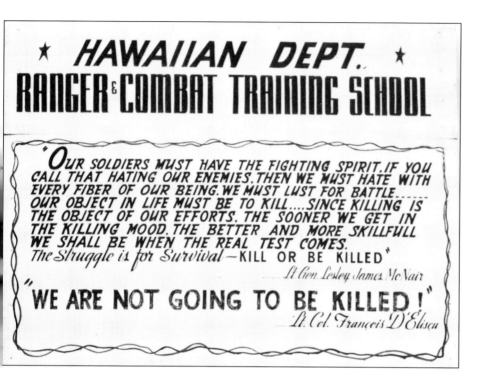

★ **HAWAIIAN DEPT.** ★
RANGER & COMBAT TRAINING SCHOOL

"OUR SOLDIERS MUST HAVE THE FIGHTING SPIRIT. IF YOU CALL THAT HATING OUR ENEMIES. THEN WE MUST HATE WITH EVERY FIBER OF OUR BEING. WE MUST LUST FOR BATTLE........ OUR OBJECT IN LIFE MUST BE TO KILL....SINCE KILLING IS THE OBJECT OF OUR EFFORTS. THE SOONER WE GET IN THE KILLING MOOD. THE BETTER AND MORE SKILLFULL WE SHALL BE WHEN THE REAL TEST COMES. The Struggle is for Survival — KILL OR BE KILLED"

...........Lt. Gen. Lesley James McNair

"WE ARE NOT GOING TO BE KILLED!"

Lt. Col. François D'Eliscu

awaii was a perfect training ground for the men who would be fighting in the Pacific, because the island terrain and climate were similar to what they would encounter elsewhere in battling the Japanese.

More than 300,000 soldiers went through the Jungle Training Centers, which taught crucial, sometimes vicious techniques to insure that Americans would be the ones to survive in confrontations with the enemy.

"Rear approach strangle hold is practiced by the men, and it's no sissy stuff as they learn the grim reality of 'kill or be killed' in jungle training school..."

The training was tough; six men died doing it.

Another important procedure for Pacific-bound soldiers to learn before they left for battle was the amphibious landing. On island beaches, *"the men go through all the backbreaking work of an amphibious operation, first in slow tempo, but gradually increasing their pace to that of actual combat..."*

Casualties

From the very first day of the war, Hawaii was faced with casualties in numbers that had never been dealt with before. As the fighting progressed, thousands more wounded were brought in from throughout the battlefronts of the Pacific. To care for them all, the Army built a number of new hospitals and also took over three schools - Farrington High School, St. Louis College, and the Kamehameha School for Girls - to turn into makeshift medical facilities. (Tripler Hospital's familiar pink structure was begun in 1944 but was not completed until four years later.) In the meantime, Aiea Naval Hospital grew to be *"considerably larger than most big city hospitals"* with *"equipment so up-to-date as to be practically unobtainable in present-day civilian hospitals;"* it saved the lives of almost every one of the over 10,000 wounded it received from the Marianas and Iwo Jima battles. As the patients recovered, they could choose from a wide range of rehabilitation activities, ranging from bowling and tennis to work in the laundry or outdoors on a farm.

Not every serviceman was as lucky. Of the more than 40,000 island men in the armed forces, 806 died.

"I remember...we had a party for my brother's friends in the Navy. There was Bill who loved to sing...there was also Duke with his unusual sense of humor...they all left on their ship, the 'Lexington,' the next morning. They never returned."

Facing page: Brig. Gen. Wayne Smith presents three posthumous awards to Mr. and Mrs. Magoichi Takeba for the heroism of their son, Sgt. Masaharu Takeba. He died on January 9, 1944 in Italy. *Above: "Here's the greatest mass decorating ceremony in history...when 141 men were decorated...for acts of heroism during the Dec. 7 attack..."* Convalescent wounded receive medals at Hickam Field on April 10, 1942. *Right:* One of Hawaii's 2,200 disabled veterans, Yoshino Omiya is led by his seeing-eye dog Audrey across busy Bishop Street in downtown Honolulu on May 2, 1945. Omiya's new postwar career was that of a masseur.

President Roosevelt came to town in July 1944, and in spite of the wartime censorship that prevented any public announcement of his presence, everybody found out anyway.

The purpose of the chief executive's visit was to hold a top-level gathering with two generals and three admirals to plan strategy in the war against Japan. The meetings were held in the same location where President Roosevelt stayed: the Queen's Surf estate of millionaire Chris Holmes.

Newspapers and radios never said a word on the subject, but even so, the stopover *"developed into a well-known secret..."*

As usual, all sorts of stories immediately sprang up:

"Rumors, speculations. Chiang Kai-shek's here, Stalin's here, Churchill's here - hail, hail, the gang's all here."

Some skeptics doubted the whole thing -

"One woman went so far as saying she saw President Roosevelt...with her own eyes! How people can lie! Blame it on wartime."

But people really did see him. FDR was driven extensively around Oahu to view the many military bases, so civilians had a chance to watch for his motorcade.

"When word magically spread that the President's party was to pass a certain corner, crowds waited patiently for hours just to get a fleeting glimpse..." One woman who did thought that *"President Roosevelt's face [was] considerably thinner and older-looking than on his last visit to Hawaii ten years ago."*

This was perhaps understandable - the president had only 9 months more to live.

A Presidential Visit

Facing page above: President Roosevelt, identifiable by his *"famous Panama hat,"* views Oahu from an elegant Packard convertible sedan. *Left:* The presidential motorcade sweeps up the driveway of St. Louis College in Kaimuki, which was serving as the Army's 147th General Hospital at that point. *Above:* *"Tokyo is the target of Admiral Chester N. Nimitz's pointer"* as Gen. Douglas MacArthur, President Roosevelt, and Adm. William Leahy look on during their Waikiki conferences.

"The main topic of conversation is, 'have you seen President Roosevelt?'"

When not on duty, the soldier, sailor, and marine faced the problem of what to do for fun. Honolulu was not a very big city in those days and its facilities were overwhelmed by these men:

"Hoping to find some of the lure and charm they'd read about, all most of them have been able to find are thousands of other fellows vaguely in search of the same thing. The consensus is it's a terrible town."

"[The men] walk up and down the streets looking for some kind of entertainment which does not exist. Poor fellows!" But there was fun to be had, even if the pickings were sometimes pretty slim.

Facing page: GIs on bicycles stop for a rest by the famous Kau Kau Korner sign, which marked the well known drive-in restaurant at Kalakaua Avenue and Kapiolani Boulevard, in 1942. ***Above:*** The landmark Wo Fat Chinese restaurant on Maunakea Street was very popular with servicemen. ***Left:*** Caroline Casimero and Pvt. Charles Carr take a turn on roller skates at the Waikiki Skating Arena at the intersection of McCully Street and Kalakaua Avenue.

The Recreation Situation

The Recreation Situation
Souvenirs for Servicemen

Honolulu became a honkytonk town as servicemen passing through seized their last opportunity to have a good time in the city [and] spend some...money... Clip joints mushroomed; you could win a dime souvenir if you paid two bits and then knocked all the bottles down; you could have your picture made with or without hula-girl embrace; you could get tattooed, or buy a set of dirty pictures."

There were no tourists anymore; yet merchants were happy with the clientele they had.

"Souvenir hunters still stalk their game in Hawaii, but now they are khaki-clad...[and] can be sold almost anything...as long as it has Hawaii on it, the men will buy it and pay any price."

Downtown Honolulu retailing undoubtedly reached its peak volume of customers in the early '40s. The amount of merchandise laid in for these potential buyers (and the subsequent slowdown after they left) can be judged by the unsold wartime souvenirs that could still be purchased there more than forty years later.

Above: A bracelet for the girl he left behind. *Left:* There were all sorts of goodies to grab a guy's paycheck..."*And then there are THOSE silk pillow tops! Shades of the D.T.'s! Works of art if ever there was. Delicately tinted in the worst color combinations conceivable...*" *Facing page:* Customers look over a display case containing wallet sized nude pin-ups.

EVEN **SNAFU** KNOWS.... **V.D.** CAN BE PREVENTED!

DON'T GET BURNED...USE COVER
CLOSE COVER BEFORE STRIKING

The Recreation Suituation

Prostitution In Paradise

New **SENATOR HOTEL** 121 NORTH HOTEL ST. HONOLULU, T.H.

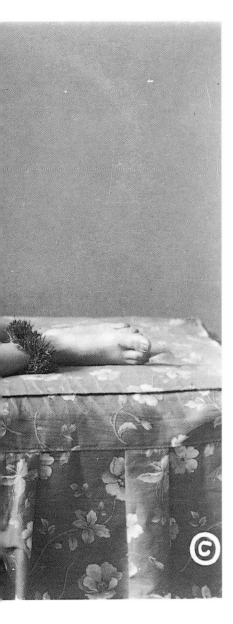

Organized prostitution had been considered necessary even before the war, due to a large population of single male plantation workers - and then the armed forces descended on the islands with even more single men. The result: the world's oldest profession boomed.

Prostitution was illegal in Hawaii, but as in many mainland locations in that period it was allowed to exist within limits. The police department regulated the trade and registered the women who worked at it, and in Honolulu confined it to a prescribed red light district between River, Kukui, Nuuanu and South Hotel Streets. This area boasted 20 to 25 "hotels" (as they were euphemistically known,) like the Bell Rooms ("Give The Bell A Ring"), The Bungalow, and the Ritz, Bronx, and Senator Hotels - the last probably being the most famous. The houses functioned so openly that *"the lines wound around the blocks occupied by certain...establishments..."* and every Honolulu citizen knew full well what the men were waiting for. Once inside, a customer paid $3 to $5 for up to four minutes of presumed pleasure; if he failed to get satisfaction, he'd receive a raincheck for a later date. Even at such bargain rates, the high turnover and huge clientele meant individual girls earned about $25,000 a year and their madams as much as $150,000; the whole take was equal to the amount generated by the tourist industry before the war! Prostitutes were notorious big spenders, and could buy whatever they wanted - in most cases. One tried to talk a tire rationing board reviewer into giving her clearance for a difficult-to-get new auto tire. He asked:

"...why couldn't she come to town on the bus[?] Too many people knew her and whistled at her! Quite a clientele...He turned her down. What did she do? Went and bought a new car, and put its tires on her own job. Then demanded her allowance from the gas rationers."

Prostitution spread from downtown to apartments and homes throughout the city, into residential neighborhoods like Waikiki and St. Louis Heights. The police cracked down; the prostitutes went on strike and

picketed the office of the military governor - who, according to some people, had arranged to ship a number of the women into Hawaii in the first place.

But the end was near. The Maui houses had been closed in April 1942; Kauai's in April 1944, and *"September 21, 1944 was a red-letter day [in Honolulu] in regard to our red light district. On that date the houses of prostitution were closed by the police at the request of Governor Stainback."*

This action was not met with universal approval.

"...if the sexual desires of men in this predominately masculine community are going to be satisfied...[we would] rather see them satisfied in regulated brothels than by our own young girls and women..."

People were fearful; stories of dangerous military men on the loose abounded. One young woman carried a gun (unloaded) on the car seat next to her if she had to drive at night; a man wrote that *"My eight-year-old niece...is not permitted to go to the store alone anymore. Every time she [does], a sailor or soldier tries to get smart with her...So the best thing...is to keep her at home...so we can avoid a rape case..."*

In fact, rapes actually decreased in number, as did the cases of venereal diseases. What did increase were the rates charged by the prostitutes still in business, which zoomed to $100.

Facing page: Although not a prostitute, this perky pin-up girl represents what the armed forces hoped to encounter in Hawaii. Below her, matchbooks tell very different stories: bumbling Private Snafu, a cartoon character whose exploits showed GIs what **not** to do, runs from the threat of VD - picked up at places like the Senator Hotel, and others.

The Recreation Situation
Hawaii Meets The Military

"We are proud to entertain in our homes the men who have been or are about to do the actual fighting of the war."

There are a lot of civilians on the Islands. Most of them were here before...Pearl Harbor. And they have every intention of staying when we GI's go home."

Of necessity, military and civilians rubbed shoulders - with varying degrees of compatibility - all throughout the war. There was one big problem for the newcomers:

"Girls are scarce in Hawaii...there simply aren't enough wahines (gals) to go around. Sooner or later...you'll get around to what philosophers call 'Acceptance'[of this.]"

On the other hand, single women found the situation a bonanza, although it could be tiring.

"Hawaii is a heaven for girls. Dates, dates, dates and more dates from service-men..."

"Various guesses have been made as to the ratio of men to women and [it] seems to be about 250 to 1...it is not strange to see one woman dining out with four or five officers."

And there was more than just "dining out" going on, with husbands and wives separated by war. Divorce rates almost doubled; and illegitimate births increased as well.

"Some Japanese girls believe it is 'patriotic' to have babies of our white soldiers. That's what a Japanese girl student of the University of Hawaii told me..."

On a more casual level, the average soldier or sailor liked to meet and just get to know residents. Many of them, in turn, were hospitable.

"I like to entertain soldiers and sailors because I feel that somebody, somewhere is entertaining a soldier or sailor who could

easily be my own brother or a close relative."

The men who were able to visit local families were appreciative; as one sailor wrote to his hosts:

"It was very kind of you to invite two men into your home that you knew nothing about. It was very fortunate for me that I was one of the lucky ones."

Unfortunately, the overwhelming quantity of servicemen in Hawaii meant that most could not be as lucky. For them there was *"homesickness and loneliness that nothing can cure but a walk down the Main Street of their home town after the war is over."*

Facing page: Bam Sperry and six sailors form a patriotic "V For Victory;" February 1942. *Above:* Military and civilian alike enjoy a luau - *except* for the girl standing in back!

The Recreation Situation

The USO

The armed services had facilities for recreation in many locations, and these were augmented by the United Service Organizations - the USO. Starting in early 1942, USO locations were opened all throughout the islands in buildings as diverse as former stores, auto showrooms, church buildings, private homes, and closed Japanese language schools. Decorating and furnishings were often donated by the public. The USOs varied greatly in size and in what they offered, but the 8,000 volunteer workers always made servicemen welcome.

Facing page: In March 1945, men relax at the Wailuku, Maui USO. *Above:* Army men who'd spent a year or more in a forward location could rest at the Kilauea Military Camp on the Big Island, where *"...the staff of Red Cross girls...act as hostesses and dancing partners at the Saturday night dances..."* *Left:* The USO in Honokaa, on the Big Island, was a former movie theater.

ROYAL
HAWAIIAN

RETURN
PASS

MAY
19

Far above: Some of the Royal Hawaiian's 200,000 wartime Naval guests relax behind a seaside barbed wire fence. *Above:* A hotel pass used by wartime military "guests". *Right:* Four Army nurses check out Waikiki while other beachgoers check out *them*; July 1945.

The Recreation Situation
Wartime Waikiki

Thousands of tourists had played at Waikiki - but now there were none, since the Navy controlled travel to and from Hawaii and did not allow pleasure trips. So instead, thousands of military personnel came to enjoy the famous beach during their time off. It was not the same Waikiki as before the war, though; barbed wire barricades now lined its sands, and there were other changes too. Fort DeRussy became a huge recreation center, with a dance hall called Maluhia that attracted thousands of men at a time. The Moana Hotel continued to function, but many other establishments and private homes in the area were taken over by the military - most notably, the Royal Hawaiian Hotel.

"The same coral-pink castle can [still] be seen...nestling amidst the world's most beautiful hotel gardens - but it is no longer the Royal Hawaiian Hotel. It is the R. and R. Annex, Submarine Base, Pearl Harbor; rest and recreation."

Instead of the former guests who'd attended *"brilliant social affairs"* there, now *"sailors, with something like poetic justice, sleep in one-time $40 and $50 suites for 25¢ a night."*

Below: Army men and women enjoy the beach at Fort DeRussy, the Army's major recreation area.

"[The Royal Hawaiian] now serves primarily the U.S.Navy, but army personnel find rest and recreation here, too."

The Recreation Situation
A Hula For The Boys

"Now, if you see a pretty Hawaiian girl wearing a grass skirt and dancing some form of the Hula, go easy. She may be a graduate of the University of Hawaii with a Ph. D. in - the dance."

Facing page: "Miss Leo Lani" gets wistful stares at the 7th Fighter Command party. *Right:* A sailor makes some tentative moves as he receives a hula lesson. *Below:* A period postcard comments on the military audience's reactions.

IT'S NOT EASY TO DO EH BUD?

ALOHA HAWAII, U.S.A.

The troops and war workers of Hawaii wanted entertainment, but often it was impossible for these men to attend any sort of show; either they were stuck in some out-of-the-way encampment, or their work schedule was too tight.

"This problem...has been a very real one for the Army in Hawaii. But [it] has been neatly solved...in cooperation with the USO."

Traveling shows were the answer, and often these were Hawaii's own homegrown hula troupes.

The Recreation Situation

Showtime In The Islands

T he hula troupes, though doing their best, were far too few in number...From this it became evident - the hula was not enough."

Local entertainers alone couldn't handle all the new audiences in wartime Hawaii, so to fill the gap the USO and the armed services themselves put on shows of all types. Mostly these were small individual troupes of musicians and comedians of varying talents, but there were also plays and musical reviews with scores of performers. And, from time to time, some really big names came through to give shows for the boys in uniform that civilians were usually not invited to.

"Maurice Evans of Shakespearean fame is here...not long ago he gave a recital..Artie Shaw is here too, but I don't care for his type of music."

Facing page: Hollywood comes to Hawaii - from left, actress Carole Landis at Aiea Naval Hospital, Bob Hope (who else?) on Kauai, and singer Betty Hutton at Kaneohe Naval Air Station.

Far above: Famous bandleader Artie Shaw with his Navy band, at Pearl Harbor; and *above,* hijinks on stage during "Girl Crazy," a USO show, at the Waipio Amphibious Base at Pearl Harbor.

The Recreation Situation
R & R

None of them say much, these boys...they're years older than they were last year..."

The men who had been on hazardous duty on the front lines of the Pacific needed a respite from the fatiguing traumas of war that seemed to age them prematurely. In recognition of their efforts, they were offered rest and relaxation in some of Hawaii's special places. When these aircraft pilots and submariners were on leave they got to stay at separate R & R camps, or sometimes in private homes. Two hundred civilian families throughout the islands, mostly wealthy, hosted tired servicemen by putting them up (at the homeowner's expense) for a minimum of 5 days. During this time the guests were entertained with various planned activities, or allowed to relax as they wished. For those not lucky enough to stay in such surroundings, there were still officers clubs at different beaches that were a calming influence after the experience of battle.

Facing page: Boy (a Navy pilot) meets girl on a Hawaiian beach during R & R; February 1944. *Left:* A local girl demonstrates the eating of one-finger poi for another Navy flier at a luau at the Queen's Surf estate of Chris Holmes in March 1944. *Below:* Men returned from the battlegrounds of the Pacific relax by playing billiards at the Commissioned Officers Beach Club in Kaneohe.

VICTORY!

For the first two years [of the war] there was...excitement...[but] as the combat areas receded...the glamor began to recede, leaving only the inconveniences of overcrowding, still-necessary restrictions and work."

By 1945 people were tired and worn out.

"*I fail to see any excitement...around town over the fall of Germany,*" wrote one man in May of that year, mindful that the Pacific war was still very much on. Local residents were happy, but V-E Day in Hawaii didn't produce the ecstatic pandemonium that it did in some other places.

But finally, in August, the Japanese admitted they too were ready to give up. Starting August 10th, people eagerly grabbed newspapers and hovered near radios to catch the definite word. There were two false alarms...but finally, at 1:42 p.m. on August 14, 1945, it was really and truly over. PEACE!

At long last, with fireworks and car horns and air raid sirens and gas alarm gongs and church bells, Hawaii's greatest and most heartfelt celebration burst forth. In downtown Honolulu, torn-up paper was flung from office buildings onto the mobbed streets. While some people headed for church, many others headed for bars. Businesses closed, and with an overwhelming sense of relief, everyone took the next day off as well.

Upper right: At Pearl Harbor, the Navy hears the radio announcement of Japan's surrender! *Right:* A typical scene in downtown Honolulu on the afternoon of August 14, 1945. *Facing page:* Jubilant newspaper buyers react to the *Honolulu Advertiser's* headline.

"Drove thru town and could hardly get home. I never believed my car could carry so many sailors and soldiers at one time...Fun? Well, I can truthfully say that I was never happier in all my life!"

Winding Up The War

The postwar world brought adjustments. No more shortages! Available at last: *"LUX! Swan Soap!...paper clips... extension cords...fresh MEAT!...Gasoline... unrationed tires...Sparkling white new washing machines for **sale**... Mainland liquor..."*

Some aspects of the war vanished quickly: *"Rusting bits of barbed wire half-buried in the sand [are] all that's left of Oahu's defensive barricade!"*

Other changes: as thousands of servicemen and war workers were shipped out, island members of the military were returning, along with residents who'd evacuated to the mainland or had been caught there when the war started. Land taken over by the military was returned (in most cases) to its owners and the formerly crowded camps and training centers were left empty.

Not so obvious as all this, though, were the fundamental changes World War II brought to Hawaii's people. The stratified and controlled prewar society had been shaken up, never to return. Local Japanese veterans would be in the forefront of a political changeover that would that would take years to evolve, but the roots of the movement would remain in the wartime disruptions that broke up Hawaii's previously existing class system.

"No one...expects to see the Territory ever to return exactly to the conditions that prevailed here before the war."

Facing page: Sgt. Shige Fukuda regards his discharge from the famous 442nd Regiment after a ceremony at Kapiolani Park on August 15, 1946; girlfriend Edna Oda sits at his side. ***This page, first column above:*** Gen. Francis Englehart and Capt. Spencer Tinker inspect a row of Army autos to be sold as surplus in October 1945. ***Below:*** An air raid shelter at Lincoln School is burned before being bulldozed. ***Second column top:*** Cpl. Carey Pruitt shows off a $25 war bond belonging to Mrs. Joseph Lawelawe that he found among gas masks returned to the Army by the public. ***Middle:*** A civilian worker locks the doors of the Office of Radio and Cable Censorship for the last time. ***Bottom:*** A legacy of the war - Army Bomb Disposal Squad men stand next to a Japanese mine that washed up at Paia, Maui in January 1948. Live wartime explosives are still sometimes found, more than forty years later. ***Previous pages:*** A joyous scene in downtown Honolulu on surrender day.

Those Who Fell

The excitement of war's end was tempered with a respectful awareness of those who were gone. More than eight hundred of Hawaii's men died, in locations all over the world. After the war many of their bodies were returned to the islands, and along with them came the dead from battles throughout the Pacific. Temporary cemeteries had been established in different areas of Oahu during the war, starting with the victims of the Pearl Harbor attack, and eventually all these remains were brought together at the National Memorial Cemetery of the Pacific at Punchbowl Crater in Honolulu.

Development of the cemetery began in 1948 and the first burials took place in January of the following year. A large memorial structure, completed in 1962, lists the names of the missing from World War II and other wars that followed, and wall maps display the battlegrounds on which American servicemen fought and died.

Each Memorial Day, every grave at Punchbowl receives a lei, insuring that none of the war dead - from World War II on - is forgotten.

Facing page: At Punchbowl Crater on Memorial Day 1952, Mrs. Agnes Bickerton places a cross of white plumeria blossoms on the grave of her son Bud, who died in Tunisia in April 1943. ***Right:*** The remains of men killed in battles on Saipan, Guam, Truk, Kwajalein, Guadalcanal, and other Pacific islands await processing at a Schofield Barracks mausoleum in March 1948. Probably most would be interred at Punchbowl.

The Arizona Memorial

The Japanese attack of December 7th left the USS Arizona on the bottom of Pearl Harbor with many of her crew still on board - almost half of all the American military deaths of the raid. While repair work went on all around her, the Arizona remained untouched until the superstructure of the ship, still well above water level, was removed for salvage in 1943. The hull remained as it was.

As early as 1944, ideas for a Pearl Harbor memorial began to be publicized. Military leaders, civilian city planners, and many others made differing suggestions as to what might be appropriate - a monument, an auditorium, a grove of trees - and where the memorial ought to be situated. The discussions continued for years; but in the meantime, after the war, thoughts of raising the Arizona were permanently dropped.

In the 1950s a small wooden structure was built over the hull of the ship with a flagpole and commemorative plaque. Only special visitors were landed on this simple platform; all others simply viewed the scene from passing boats.

Later in that decade, planning got underway for a larger structure. $500,000 was needed for the construction of the Arizona Memorial; $65,000 of this sum came from a special concert given by Elvis Presley in March 1961. Six months later, work began; by May 30, 1962 the current Arizona Memorial was completed. The onshore visitor center followed in October 1980.

The Arizona Memorial was designed by architect Alfred Preis, a Hawaii resident originally from Austria. Ironically, Preis had been imprisoned in a local internment camp along with some other Europeans (and, of course, many Japanese) at the beginning of the war, since he and his wife still held German passports and had not yet become naturalized American citizens.

What today's visitor sees at Pearl Harbor is a serene white monument with a silhouette that dips in the middle, with openings in the walls and roof that admit views of the Hawaiian sky. The rusting body of the Arizona, still easily seen below, occasionally leaks a droplet of oil that spreads across the tradewind-ruffled surface of Pearl Harbor. Within that hull are the 1,177 victims of the attack which remains a crucial event in the history of the United States and the entire world.

Hawaii has seen countless changes since the war years; but unlike so much else in the islands, the Arizona Memorial as it now stands is unlikely to be altered. It will remain the focal point of Hawaii's remembrances of the tremendously varied experiences of World War II.

Facing page: A Special Board of Review inspects the hull of the Arizona in March 1948 to determine whether the ship should be raised and the remains of her crew removed. *Left:* The Arizona Memorial under construction in March 1962. The flagpole to the left marks the earlier, temporary wooden platform that was removed when the present structure was completed. *Below:* Sailors salute the USS Arizona from the flight deck of the nuclear powered aircraft carrier USS Carl Vinson as it enters Pearl Harbor on May 16, 1986.

PHOTO CREDITS

Honolulu:

Bishop Museum: 2, 64, 88, 89 (below), 123 (below, both), 125 (below), 145 (below). *Ray Jerome Baker:* 15, 55 (below), 60 (below), 131 (above). *Yew Char:* 23. *R. Fujimoto:* 104-105. *Tai Sing Loo:* 137, 143 (above),145 (above). *Miura Collection:* 65.

Hawaii State Archives: 8-9, 10-11, 13, 48-49, 50-51 (above), 51 (lower right), 54, 59 (below), 103, 114, 115 (below), 126, 127 (above), 157 (above). *Admiral Furlong Collection:* 86 (lower left), 107 (above).

Hawaii War Records Depository, University of Hawaii: Cover, 16 (lower left), 44-45, 55 (above), 55-56, 57 (both), 59 (above), 62 (above), 63, 66, 68, 70, 74 (upper left), 74-75, 76, 80, 81, 82, 83 (below), 86 (lower right), 91, 92, 94, 95 (all), 96, 97 (both), 101 (both), 102, 105, 108 (above), 109, 110 (both), 111, 112-113, 116-117, 121 (above), 131 (below), 133, 136, 148 (below), 152, 153 (bottom center).

Honolulu Advertiser: 58, 157 (below).

Honolulu Star-Bulletin: 46 (above), 71 (above), 83 (above).

Author's collection: 4-5, 6, 11 (far right, both), 17 (lower right), 52 (both), 67, 69, 134-135 (all), 140 (lower left), 143 (below). *Turner & DeVries photos:* Endpapers, 10 (left), 14 (right), 16-17, 33, 53 (all), 62 (below), 71 (below), 75 (right), 84, 85 (below), 89 (above), 104 (below), 108 (below), 132 (both). *Photo by author:* 48 (collection of Lawrence M. Judd.)

Mike Mauricio: 14 (collection of Mrs. Kimi Fujioka).

Washington, D. C.:

Department of Defense Still Media Depository, U.S.Army: 12-13, 20 (above), 21, 22, 24, 25, 26, 27, 28, 29, 35 (lower right), 37,
42-43, 46 (below), 47, 50-51(below), 60 (above), 77, 78, 79 (both), 86-87, 90, 93, 98, 99, 107 (below), 112 (below), 113, 119, 120, 121 (below), 122-123, 124, 127 (below), 129 (upper right), 130, 138, 139 (above), 140 (lower right), 141, 142, 144 (center), 149, 153 (all except bottom center), 154, 155, 156. **U.S.Marine Corps:** 118, 122, 125 (above), 139 (below).

Library of Congress: 31 (Navy), 115 (above; Army).

National Archives, U.S.Navy: 18-19, 20 (above), 34-35, 36, 38-39, 40-41, 42, 60-61, 85 (above) 100, 106, 128 (upper left), 128-129, 140 (above), 144 (left, right), 146-147 (all), 148 (above), 150-151.

Cover photo handtinted by Ron Hudson.

QUOTE CREDITS

All quotes are listed from top to bottom, and left to right. Abbreviations stand for the following sources:

Adv   *Honolulu Advertiser*
SB   *Honolulu Star-Bulletin*
POP   *Paradise of the Pacific* magazine
Haw   *Hawaii* magazine
UH   Hawaii War Records Depository, University of Hawaii
ML   diary of Manuel Lemes, Hawaii War Records Depository, University of Hawaii

     Dear diary: I still don't know why I keep a diary. Oh, well! some day, somebody may probably enjoy reading it. [Diary of Manuel Lemes, May 16, 1944]

     *It is a favorable record that the files of Hawaii War Records Depository reveal...*The Hawaii War Records Depository is housed in Hamilton Library, University of Hawaii. It contains a great variety of written material, including personal letters, excepts from diaries, transcribed interviews and reminiscences, school compositions, agency files and reports, and clippings from different periodicals. These are listed first by the name of the writer (if known), and then either the type of item or its title, if any.

     Articles that are quoted repeatedly have their titles abbreviated after the first listing.

     If consecutive quotes are from the same source, the source will be noted only before the first quote.

7   **POP**, "Peace and Rumors of War in the Pacific", Jan. 1936.

16   **Haw**, "News – Prospect and Retrospect", Nov. 29, 1941.

17   1) **Adv**, "Christmas Spirit", Dec. 2, 1941; **Haw**, 2) "News...", Apr. 30, 1941; 3) "Rising Sun Spreads Its Rays", Sept. 13, 1941; 4) **POP**, Hawaii Tourist Bureau ad, Dec. 1941.

20   **UH**: 1) Robert Au, "Dec. 7, 1941"; 2) Joan Irene Stidham, "Under Attack"; 3) Clara L. Chapin, "Personal Experiences of Kamehameha School for Girls During the Dec. 7th Attack and The Days Following"; 4) Grace Tower Warren, "War In Paradise"; 5) Mrs. Robert Thompson, "Observations Made December 7, 1941".

22   **UH**, A. A. Kempa, diary.

23   **UH**: 1) A. A. Kempa, diary; 2) Richard Tamabayashi; 3) Toraichi Kagihara.

24   **UH**: Irwin Spalding, letter, Mar. 1, 1942.

26   **UH**: Betty Wong, "The Closest Feeling To War"; 2) Mrs. Robert Thompson, "Observations Made December 7, 1941"; 3) A. A. Kempa, diary; 4) Mrs. T. K. Whitelaw, letter, Mar. 1942; 5) Fuyunori Kaito, "Destruction at Dawn"; 6) Henry Higa.

27   **UH**, Susie Lee, "December 7th".

29   **UH**, Mrs. T. K. Whitelaw, letter, Mar. 1942.

30   **UH**: 1) Hilda Eliasson; 2) Grace Hunter; 3) Stephen Moon, "I Whitnessed A Murder".

32   **UH**: 1) Mrs. Lillian Williams, "I Wrote This On December 7th, 1941"; 2) Mrs. Albert S. Stevens, "That Day of Pearl Harbor", **Harpers**, Jan. 1943; 3) Violet K. Kinney, letter, Dec. 22, 1941; 4) Elmer Anderson, **The Whitewater Register** [Wisc.], Mar. 19, 1942; 5) Robert Teruya, "A Bitter Sunday"; 6) Mrs. T. K. Whitelaw, letter, Mar. 1942; 7) same as #1; 8) Mrs. Fred R. Giddings, diary, Dec. 9, 1941; 9) Robert Au, "Dec. 7, 1941"; 10) Mrs. Eric Knudsen, diary, Dec. 10, 1941;

11) Margaret Dean, letter, Dec. 7-8, 1941.

35 **UH**: 1) Edward Manner; 2) Mrs. Mary Helen Stevens.

37 **UH**: 1) Edward Manner; 2) Esther Matsukawa, "An Unforgettable Day"; 3) and 4) Harriet Estabrook.

38 **UH**: 1) Mrs. Robert Thompson, "Observations Made December 7, 1941"; 2) James A. Spagnola; 3) ML, Dec. 8, 1941.

42 1) **UH**, Edward Manner; 2) **SB**, "City Decorates Graves of Pearl Harbor Heroes", Jan. 1, 1942.

46 1) and 2) **Haw**, Ellen L. Bairos, "Memos From the Associate Editor's Desk", Dec. 1941; **UH**; 3) and 4) Mrs. T. K. Whitelaw, letter, Mar. 1942; 5) Arthur C. Alexander, "Doings of the Alexander Family In Honolulu"; 6) Mrs. Robert Thompson, "Rumors and Facts After Dec. 7"; 7) Mrs. Eric Kundsen, diary, April 12, 1942; 8) Mrs. Albert S. Stevens, "That Day of Pearl Harbor", **Harpers**, Jan. 1943; 9) same as [#]5; 10) same as [#]1; 11) **POP**, Henry Dougherty, "War Came To Hawaii", May 1942.

48 **UH**: 1) Grace Hunter; 2) ML, Dec. 15, 1941.

50 1) **UH**, Arthur C. Alexander, "Doings of the Alexander Family in Honolulu"; **Haw**: 2) "The Enemy Is Complacency!", June 30, 1942; 3) Nona Gaddis, "Lady Like", Mar. 21, 1942; 4) Ellen L. Bairos, "Notes...", Jan. 17, 1942; 5) ML, Feb. 10, 1942.

51 **UH**, Violet K. Kinney, letter, Jan. 15, 1942.

53 **POP**, "Out of the Night", Jan. 1942.

55 **UH**: 1) Mrs. T. K. Whitelaw, letter, Mar. 1942; 2) Mrs. Eric Knudsen, diary, Apr. 16, 1942.

57 1) **Haw**, Jean Parta, "Wartime Honolulu", Jan. 31, 1942; **UH**: 2) Mary E. Hall; 3) Ronald Chee, "School Life In World War II"; 4) Chieko Ginoza, "The War and My Community".

58 1) **UH**, Mrs.T. K. Whitelaw, letter, Mar. 1942; 2) **SB**, "Air Raid Warning", Mar. 7, 1942.

59 **POP**, Henry Dougherty, "War Came To Hawaii", May 1942.

60 1) **POP**, "As We See It In Hawaii", June 1942; **UH**: 2) Grace Tower Warren, "War In Paradise", Jan. 1942; 3) Mrs. Knudsen, diary, Dec. 29, 1941.

63 **UH**, Mary E. Hall.

66 **POP**, "As We See It In Hawaii", Feb. 1942.

67 1) **POP**, "Out Of The Night", Jan. 1942; **UH**: 2) Mrs. Eric Knudsen, diary, Dec. 1941; 3) ML, May 3, 1944; 4) ML, Mar. 24, 1944; 5) Helen Berkey, diary, June 2, 1942.

68 **UH**, C. E. Morris, letter, Feb. 3, 1942.

70 1) **UH**, Elmer Anderson, **The Whitewater Register** [Wisc.], Mar. 19, 1942; 2) **Adv**, "Provost Court Acts Swiftly On Civil Offenses", Dec. 10, 1941; 3) **Adv**, "Policemen Can Search Homes", Mar. I, 1942; 4) **Haw**, "If Martial Law Is Lifted...Then What?", May 1, 1944; 5) ML, Sept. 1, 1945; 6) ML, Dec. 4, 1942.

72 1) "BLACKOUT", handout, May 23, 1940; 2) "URGENT * WARNING * URGENT", handout, May 23, 1940; 3) **UH**, Richard Wrenshall, letter, Mar. 1942; 4) **UH**, Mrs. T. K. Whitelaw, letter, Mar. 1942; 5) **Haw**, Jean Parta, "Ketchup In The Butter", Dec. 1941; 6) **UH**, Mrs. Fred R. Giddings, diary, Dec. 9, 1941; 7) **Adv**, LaSelle Gilman, "Hawaii War Diary", May 2, 1942; 8) ML, Mar. 2, 1942; 9) **Haw**, "Light and Airy!", July 17, 1943; 10) **Haw**, Ellen L. Bairos, "Memos...", Mar. 1, 1944; 11) **UH**, Mrs. Eric Knudsen, diary, Dec. 9, 1941.

73 **UH**, F. D. Lowrey, letter, Nov. 2, 1942.

74 1) **POP**, "A Yank's-Eye View of Honolulu", Apr. 1944; 2) **UH**, Joan Irene Stidham, "Coed Tells of Christmas in War-Torn Hawaii, 1941", **The Lawrentian**; 3) ML, Dec. 19, 1941; 4) **UH**, Mrs. Eric Knudsen, diary, Jan. 28, 1942; 5) **POP**, Henry Dougherty, "About 6 p.m. In Honolulu", May 1942; 6) **UH**, Grace Tower Warren, "War In Paradise", 7) **UH**, Elmer Anderson, **The Whitewater Register** [Wisc.], Mar. 19, 1942; 8) [author's collection] E. White Sutton, letter, Mar. 12, 1943; 9) **Adv**, "Blackout Here For Duration, General Says", Jan. 9, 1942; 10) **Haw**, Moana Peterson Shepherd, "Musings of a Kuaaina", July-Aug. 1945; 11) same as [#]8.

76 1) **Haw**, Jean Parta, "Wartime Honolulu", Jan. 31, 1942; 2) **POP**, "Central Identification Bureau", Oct. 1944; 3) ML, May 11, 1942.

78 1) **POP**, Henry Dougherty, "War Came To Hawaii", May 1942; 2) **UH**, Dorothy Chu, "Lesson 1: The Importance of the Gas Mask"; 3) ML, Oct. 14, 1943.

79 ML, Oct. 14, 1943.

80 **Haw**, Moana Peterson Shepherd, "Musings...", July 31, 1943.

81 ML, Oct. 14, 1943.

84 1) **POP**, Lt. Alexander MacDonald, "There's Sense In Censorship", Dec. 1942; 2) ML, Dec. 3, 1944; 3) **Adv**, "Army Censors Island Mails", Dec. 18, 1941; 4) **Haw**, Edgar Rice Burroughs, "Laugh It Off", June 1945; 5) **UH**, Mary E. Hall.

85 **Haw**, Ellen L. Bairos, "Memos...", Dec. 1942.

87 1) **UH**, Virginia R. Jones, Apr. 1942; 2) **Haw**, Ellen L. Bairos, "Memos...", Dec. 1942; 3) **POP**, Bobbie Sandborn, "A New Hawaii", June 1945; 4) ML, June 13, 1945.

89 1) **POP**, Bobbie Sandborn, "A New Hawaii", June 1945; 2) **UH**, Violet K. Kinney, letter, May 22, 1942, 3) ML, Apr. 16, 1942; 4) ML, Apr. 24, 1942; 5) ML, Feb. 4, 1945; 6) **Haw**, Ellen L. Bairos, "Memos...", Mar. 1943; 7) same as [#]1; 8) **Haw**, Ellen L. Bairos, "Memos...", Dec. 1942.

91 1) **POP**, "A Needed Reminder", Oct. 1942; 2) **UH**, Albert Kashiwa, "My Part In The War Against The U.S. Army".

92 **UH**: 1) Harold Yamaguchi, "Pineapples And The War", 2) Laura Hee, "Pineapple All Around, But Not One To Eat"; 3) and 4) "Laupahoehoe High School After Dec. 7, 1941", 5) Hang-Fa Wong, "My First Day In The Canefield"; 6) Yachiyo Ishikawa, "Work In The Canefield"; 7) **SB**, Lawrence Nakatsuka, "3 High Schools Send 3,500 Into War Work", May 28, 1942; 8) **POP**, Ruth E. Black, "Youth In Wartime Hawaii", Dec. 1942; 9) **Adv**, LaSelle Gilman, "Honolulu War Diary", May 26, 1942; 10) and 11) **Haw**, "A Beginning", Mar. 17, 1944.

95 **Adv**, "Tons of Rubber Pour In On First Day", June 17, 1942.

97 1) **UH**, Mrs. T. K.Whitelaw, letter, Mar. 1942; 2) **Haw**, Pacific Guano and Fertilizer Co. ad, Jan. 17, 1942.

98 1) **Adv**, "Dogs For Defense", May 23, 1942; 2), 3), and 4) **POP**, H. K. L. Castle, "War Dogs", Dec. 1942; 5) original photo caption.

101 1) **SB**, Lawrence Nakatsuka, "3 High Schools Send 3,500 Into War Work", May 28, 1942; 2) ML, Jan. 22, 1942; 3) **POP**, " The Year In Retrospect", Dec. 1942.

103 1) and 2) **Haw**, Mike Fern, "Kauai The Unconquerable", May 20, 1942; **UH**; 2) Grace Tower Warren, "War In Paradise", 3) Dorothy Chu, "Lesson 1: The Importance Of The Gas Mask".

104 **Haw**, "The Enemy Is Complacency! June 30, 1942.

105 1) **POP**, Charles J. Henderson, "Civilian Defense In Hawaii", Dec. 1942; 2) **Haw**, "It Is The Improbable That Happens", Nov. 16, 1943.

106 1) ML, Jan. 13, 1942; 2) ML, June 3, 1943; 3) **POP**, "MUSCLES", Dec. 1942.

108 1) ML, Oct. 28, 1943; 2) **Haw**, Ellen L. Bairos, "Memos...", Feb. 14, 1942.

110 **Haw**, Watumull's East India Store ad, June 30, 1942.

112 **UH**, Clara L. Chapin, "Personal Experiences of Kamehameha School For Girls During The Dec. 7th Attack and The Days Following".

113 **SB**, "A Principle At Stake", Apr. 25, 1942; 2) **UH**, Grace Tower Warren, "War In Paradise"; 3) **Haw**, The Fair Department Store ad, Apr. 1943.

114 1) **UH**, George Izumi, "The Shifted Sand"; 2) **Adv**, Elmer Anderson, "Young Japanese Urged To Show U. S. Loyalty", Feb. 28, 1942; 3) **POP**, "Hawaii's Debt On Army Day", April 1944.

119 1) and 2) **UH**, U. S. Army, "Your Victory",

120 1) **POP**, LaSelle Gilman, "The Year In Retrospect", Dec. 1942; **POP**; 2) Willard Wilson, "Soldier And A Jukebox", Dec. 1944; 3) Flora Lee Simpson, "Order of the Calabash Cousins", Apr. 1944; 4) Bobbie Sandborn, "A New Hawaii", June 1945.

122 1) **UH**, Chieko Ginoza, "The War and My Community"; 2) **ML**, Dec. 27, 1943; 3) **UH**, U.S.O. publicity release, Mar. 14, 1945; 4) same as #1.

124 **ML**, Mar. 8, 1944.

125 **POP**: 1) "Finishing School of the South Pacific Combat Soldier", Jan. 1944; 2) "Prelude to Japan's Doom on Hawaii's Beaches", Jan. 1944.

126 1) **POP**, "Haven For Wounded Pacific Veterans", Dec. 1944; 2) **UH**, Leocadia Lui-Kwan, "Where The War Has Left Its Mark".

127 Original photo caption.

128 1) **POP**, "Editor's Notes", Sept. 1944; 2) **Haw**, Moana Peterson Shephard, "Musings...", Aug. 17, 1944; 3) **ML**, July 22, 1944; 4) same as #1; 5) same as #2.

129 1) **ML**, July 25, 1944; 2) **POP**, "Editor's Notes", Sept. 1944; 3) original photo caption.

131 1) **POP**, Ellen Davis, "U.S.O. Junior Volunteers", Oct. 1944; 2) **ML**, April 7, 1942.

132 1) **UH**, U.S. Army, "Your Victory"; 2) **POP**, Bobbie Sandborn, "A New Hawaii", June 1945; 3) **Haw**, William "Jazz" Belknap, "Honolulu Sideshow", April 1944.

135 **UH**: 1) U.S. Army, "Your Victory"; 2) Mrs. Yale Maxon, diary, May 1, 1943; 3) Hubert Brown, "The Effects of Closing Houses of Prostitution On The Community"; 4) **Haw**, "Why Talk About Prostitution?, July 31, 1944; 5) **ML**, Aug. 6, 1944.

137 1) **POP**, "The Old Order Changeth", Dec. 1942; 2) and 3) [author's collection] U.S. Army, "A Pocket Guide to Hawaii"; 4) **ML**, June 27, 1944; 5) **POP**, Bobbie Sandborn, "A New Hawaii", June 1945; 6) **ML**, April 9, 1942; 7) **ML**, July 31, 1943; 8) **UH**, H.D. Haseltine, letter, Apr. 14, 1941; 9) same as #1.

139 **POP**, H. K. Fairman, "Wartime Devotees of the Goddess Pele", June 1945.

141 **POP**: 1), 2), and 3) "As We See It In Hawaii", Mar. 1942; 3) Earl Selle, "Requiem For Night Life", Dec. 1942.

143 1) [author's collection] U.S. Army, "A Pocket Guide to Hawaii", 2) **POP**, Pfc. Willard C. Brown, "The Show Goes On – In Hawaii", Dec. 1942.

145 1) **POP**, Pfc. Daniel Alexander, "Hula Was Not Enough", Nov. 1943; 2) **UH**, Violet K. Kinney, letter, Mar. 1, 1943.

147 **POP**, Willard Wilson, "Soldier And A Jukebox", Dec. 1944.

148 1) **POP**, editorial, Dec. 1944; 2) **ML**, May 10, 1945; 3) **ML**, Aug. 14, 1945.

153 1) and 2) **Haw**, Ellen L. Bairos, "Notes...", Jan. and Feb. 1946; 3) **POP**, LaSelle Gilman, "The Year In Retrospect", Dec. 1942.

158 1) **POP**, "The History of Hawaii In World War II", Dec. 1944; 2) **ML**, May 16, 1944.